WORKING WILDERNESS

WORKING WILDERNESS

THE MALPAI BORDERLANDS GROUP AND THE FUTURE OF THE WESTERN RANGE

NATHAN F. SAYRE

RIO NUEVO PUBLISHERS
TUCSON, ARIZONA

*Part of the proceeds from sales of this book will be used for the
preservation of open space in the American West.*

Dedicated to the memory of
Jim Corbett (1933–2001)

Rio Nuevo Publishers®
P.O. Box 5250, Tucson, Arizona 85703-0250
(520) 623-9558, www.rionuevo.com

Library of Congress Cataloging-in-Publication Data

Sayre, Nathan Freeman.
Working wilderness : the Malpai Borderlands Group and the future of the western range / Nathan F. Sayre.
    p. cm.
Includes bibliographical references.
ISBN-13: 978-1-887896-81-8 (pbk.)
ISBN-10: 1-887896-81-3 (pbk.)
1. Nature conservation--New Mexico--History. 2. Nature conservation--Arizona--History. 3. Ranching--New Mexico--History. 4. Ranching--Arizona--History. 5. Malpai Borderlands Group--History. I. Title.

QH76.5.N6S29 2005
333.74'0978--dc22

2005021588

Design: Karen Schober, Seattle, Washington
On the front cover: photograph by William R. Radke.

Printed in Korea.

10 9 8 7 6 5 4 3 2 1

CONTENTS

PREFACE: SUPPRESSING A FIRE, IGNITING A COMMUNITY 6

ACKNOWLEDGMENTS 14

INTRODUCTION: THE WESTERN RANGE AND THE NEW WEST 20

CHAPTER 1: CRISIS, CONSENSUS, AND CONSERVATION 32

CHAPTER 2: GRAY RANCH 50

CHAPTER 3: GRAZING, FIRE, AND DROUGHT IN THE BORDERLANDS 70

CHAPTER 4: THE RADICAL CENTER: SCIENCE, POLITICS, AND PARTNERSHIPS 90

CHAPTER 5: BIODIVERSITY AND ENDANGERED SPECIES 106

CHAPTER 6: THE SPECTER OF SUBDIVISION 126

CHAPTER 7: AGAINST LONG ODDS 144

CONCLUSION: WORKING WILDERNESS 160

BIBLIOGRAPHIC NOTES 165

INDEX 174

LIST OF MAPS

MAP 1: LOCATION OF MALPAI BORDERLANDS GROUP PLANNING AREA 35

MAP 2: LANDOWNERSHIP IN THE MALPAI BORDERLANDS GROUP PLANNING AREA 36

MAP 3: FIRE IN THE MALPAI BORDERLANDS 119

MAP 4: RANCHES WITH CONSERVATION EASEMENTS 129

SUPPRESSING A FIRE,
IGNITING A COMMUNITY

On July 2, 1991, a fire broke out in a patch of grass near the Geronimo Trail Road, a lonely gravel track in far southeastern Arizona, closer to Mexico than to any building or town. By the next day the fire had been extinguished, having blackened about five hundred acres. It was an unremarkable event in a place where abundant lightning follows spring drought, and where the Forest Service had long responded to wildfires the way a fire department responds to a burning house. Unremarkable except for the fact that this particular fire struck at a particular place and time where a different kind of fuel was primed for ignition: a volatile mixture of people and land, history and ecology, passion and politics.

The people had lived there a long time, as much as five generations, and they had come to believe that the land needed to burn once in awhile. They urged the Forest Service to leave this one alone. It posed no threat to people or property and could not spread far because the surrounding vegetation was

of Sonora and Chihuahua; and "Group" describes the collaborative philosophy by which they have chosen to work.

too sparse to carry the flames. It wouldn't even have ignited if the rancher whose land it was on had not invested in killing the shrubs to encourage the grasses several years earlier; now, it needed a fire to keep new shrubs from getting the upper hand again. Let it burn, they said, you're wasting taxpayers' money. But the Service refused their entreaties and extinguished the fire, and in so doing ignited the community.

Fourteen years later, that new fire has grown to encompass some 800,000 acres. It is called the Malpai Borderlands Group, a not-for-profit organization composed of ranchers, scientists, public agencies, and private conservationists. "Malpai" comes from the ranch where they first convened; "Borderlands" refers to a 1,250-square-mile triangle of land, draped over the Continental Divide where Arizona and New Mexico meet the Mexican states

For its size, the Borderlands is believed to be one of the most biologically diverse places in North America, crowded with organisms from the Great Plains, the Sonoran and Chihuahuan Deserts, the Rocky Mountains, and the Sierra Madre. It contains grasslands and marshes, pine forests and creosote bush flats, mesquite bosques, oak savannas, cactus thickets, and ribbons of cottonwood. A fifty-acre piece of desert scrub here supports more species of rodents than does the entire state of Pennsylvania. One of its mountain passes is home to more kinds of reptiles and amphibians than any known site in the U.S. Over half of the bird species in North America can be found in the Chiricahua Mountains, immediately to the west, and the Gray Ranch, which forms the eastern third of the triangle, was named one of the world's "last great places" for biodiversity by The Nature Conservancy. Bighorn sheep and pronghorn antelope, mountain lions and black bears, and even an occasional jaguar can be found here. It is an area one-quarter larger than the state of Rhode Island, yet it has almost no paved roads. The human population is most easily expressed not in persons per square mile, but in square miles per person.

Literally and figuratively, the Malpai Borderlands Group burns to conserve this land: to keep it open, undeveloped, and wild, free of highways and houses. It burns to help repair the damage the land has experienced since Geronimo surrendered to the U.S. military in one of its jagged canyons back in 1886. Most broadly, the Malpai Group burns to sustain the Borderlands as a *working wilderness*: a place where wildness thrives not in the absence of human work or in spite of it, but because of it, and where thriving wildlands in turn sustain the human community that lives and works there. Superficially, this work is the same as it has been for five generations—the work of ranching, of raising cattle on the range—but it has grown to include scientific research, communications and outreach, real estate, law, wildlife biology, planning, and fire management as well. Not to mention politics. It's fair to say that some Malpai ranchers spend more time in meetings than they do in the saddle.

Simple as it may sound, this mission in fact represents an extraordinarily difficult challenge. It will take generations to achieve, if indeed it proves possible at all. But the Malpai Group has made impressive strides already. It has helped return fire to more than 300,000 acres of land. It has secured conservation easements that protect 75,760

THE MALPAI GROUP'S MISSION STATEMENT READS:

Our goal is to restore and maintain the natural processes that create and protect a healthy, unfragmented landscape to support a diverse, flourishing community of human, plant and animal life in our Borderlands region.

Together, we will accomplish this by working to encourage profitable ranching and other traditional livelihood which will sustain the open space nature of our land for generations to come.

acres of private land from subdivision and development, all acquired from willing sellers, without government assistance. It has implemented innovative measures to protect endangered species and supported cutting-edge research on fire, climate, vegetation, grazing, and wildlife. For its efforts in community-based conservation, Malpai has received awards from The Nature Conservancy, the Society for Conservation Biology, the National Fish and Wildlife Foundation, the U.S. Forest Service, and the Arizona Game and Fish Department. In 1998 Bill McDonald, the group's executive director, was awarded a "genius" fellowship by the MacArthur Foundation. Malpai has been featured in the *New York Times, Los Angeles Times, Smithsonian* and *Audubon* magazines, public television and the Discovery Channel, National Public Radio, and in the journals *Conservation Biology* and *BioScience*. In the bitterly fought contest over America's Western rangelands, the Malpai Borderlands Group is widely seen as a beacon of hope and possibility. Countless other efforts to protect Western landscapes from fragmentation and development have sprung up in recent years, inspired in some degree by the example of Malpai.

The story of the Malpai Borderlands Group comprises three broad questions. First, how did it happen at all? What created the fuel that was ignited by suppression of the Geronimo Trail fire? Second, what has the Malpai Group accomplished, and how? What has enabled it to unite scientists, landowners, agencies, and conservationists in a community-based effort to understand, protect, and enhance a large, complex landscape? And third, what are its prospects for the future? Does it hold lessons for conservation elsewhere, or is it one of a kind, an anomaly?

In terms of the first question, the Malpai Group presents a most improbable story, in which particular people and events seem to have come together in just the right mixture and sequence, as if by the kindness of fate. Individually and collectively, the members of the Malpai Group have demonstrated a remarkable aptitude for

Early portrait of the Malpai Borderlands Group, taken in the Glenns' barn, 1995. LEFT TO RIGHT: *Ed Roos, Bill Miller, Ross Humphreys, Larry Allen, Ray Turner (seated), Tom Peterson, Mike Dennis (top), Wendy Glenn, Ron Bemis (top), Warner Glenn, Don Dwyer (seated), Ben Brown (top), Mary McDonald, Joe Austin (middle), Billy Darnell (top), Bill McDonald (standing), John Cook (top), Drum Hadley, Seth Hadley.*

Diamond A Outfit cowboys from Cochise County, Arizona, 1880s.

turning chance events—such as Warner Glenn's 1996 encounter with a jaguar—into opportunities for achievement. Given what has been accomplished already—the answers to question two—one might easily see Malpai as a contemporary Western, complete with leather-skinned cowboys taking bold risks and arriving at a happy ending. However, question three reveals that this story is far from over, and that if it is to end happily it will have to become the first of many similar stories elsewhere. Not that the Malpai story can be copied in any simple manner—no, those stories will have to emerge from the grass roots, like the Malpai Group did, respecting and adapting to particular places, people, histories, and landscapes. Malpai can be an example and inspiration for others, but it cannot work as a model to be imposed on them.

The Malpai Group is still far from its goals, and ultimately its success or failure may depend on what happens to the rest of the West's rangelands. To appreciate the magnitude of the work that remains to be done, one must understand the strength and depth of the forces arrayed in the other direction: the economic, political, ecological, and social trends that are squeezing ranchers throughout the West and giving rise to new patterns of land use.

It may seem infinitely improbable, even miraculous, that fire broke out where it did that day in 1991, igniting that particular patch of grass and, in turn, catalyzing the Malpai Group. This perception is inside out, however. Drought follows rain in the Southwest, and lightning follows drought. Fires are a natural and inevitable result. What requires explanation, then, is not the fire that happened but the century without significant fires that preceded it—and the consequent notion that fires are somehow exceptional. Similarly, what is truly odd about the Malpai Group is not its existence or its good fortune but its rarity—the fact that it stands out so starkly against "normal" experience. It is the norm, not the exception, that cries out for explanation in this case. Virtually everyone supports the goal of conservation in the West. If it is to be realized, efforts and achievements like the Malpai Group's will have to become as unremarkable as a July fire, and vice-versa.

Geronimo Trail Road in San Bernardino Valley, near the site of the 1991 fire.

ACKNOWLEDGMENTS

This book is the partially unintended outgrowth of a series of events that began in the fall of 2001. I received a phone call one evening from Bill McDonald, who told me that the board of the Malpai Group had decided to undertake a comprehensive evaluation of what they were doing and what they should do in the next ten years or so. They wanted a big-picture evaluation, one that would identify issues they were overlooking or weak spots that might turn into Achilles' heels. The idea of a "long-term plan" was not Bill's—he admitted he personally wasn't wild about it, in fact—but if it was going to happen he wanted me to do it. Was I interested?

I jumped at the chance. For five years I had been studying ranching and environmentalism in the Southwest: the history and ecology, myths and misunderstandings of a long and nasty battle over "nature." I'd talked to a rancher who claimed Al Gore was selling Yellowstone to the Japanese, and to an environmentalist who said that talking with a

rancher would be like talking to "a guy who just raped my wife and daughter and burned down my house." The more research I did, the more I came to expect not just hyperbole and stridency but willful distortion and outright mendacity, not from one side or the other but from at least some (and sometimes many) people on all sides, including government agencies. Meanwhile, ranches all around me were turning into subdivisions: tract houses on the edges of cities, golfing and retirement communities a little further out, ten- or twenty- or forty-acre lots for speculative investors pretty much anywhere. Real estate signs seemed to dot every roadside, even where the roads weren't paved. It seemed obvious that the venomous hatred between ranchers and environmentalists was only helping to divide and conquer both.

Plenty of people recognized this, of course, but recognizing it and changing it were two very differ-

ent challenges. Getting ranch owners, environmentalists, and government officials to sit down and talk to each other was doable—indeed, everyone seemed to be doing it—but all the facilitators and flipcharts and break-out sessions did not easily carry over to actual results on the ground. Someone would misinterpret something and take offense, or slip back into accusations and distrust, or invoke some bureaucratic rule that scuttled an initiative. On a ranch tour, biologists and environmentalists would seize their binoculars to birdwatch while the host was speaking, breaking an unwritten code of hospitality and good behavior among ranchers; the rancher, in turn, would suspect them of looking for an endangered species. The combination of lawsuits, rising property values, inadequate science, and rigid procedures seemed insurmountable.

I had been to the Gray Ranch and I'd seen several people from the Malpai Group speak at conferences and workshops. I didn't know much about them, but it was obvious that somehow, they had defused the ideological warfare in a way that translated into concrete results. The results reinforced everyone's commitment and built up enthusiasm for further challenges. The difference was striking but elusive—as though they were breathing different air or something. I wanted to find out how they'd done it. If I could do it at their invitation and help them out in the process, so much the better.

For the next two years I tracked down all the reports, studies, memoirs, and archives I could find relating to the Borderlands and to Malpai's mission. I attended meetings and interviewed Malpai members, cooperators, and people who had played key roles at one point or another. I wrote a state-of-the-knowledge review of the social and ecological issues bearing on Malpai's mission, and then the plan itself. Several months later, I was asked to present a summary to the Science Advisory Committee, a group of two or three dozen biologists and ecologists who volunteer to advise the Group. There should be a book, they said, that puts all this information in one place, where people can get it. A few minutes later, I had been volunteered for the job.

One could not hope to write such a book without the active participation and support of the Malpai Group, and in hiring me to write the long-term plan the Group supported roughly half of the research involved. This book was written independently, however; it is an authorized and invited history (or biography?) of the Malpai Group but not a commissioned one. The long-term plan was conceived as a critical evaluation: the point was to look for weaknesses or places where the Group could improve. Had I felt pressured to produce predetermined results in the plan, I would not have agreed to tackle this book, which like the plan seeks to provide a candid, independent account.

I am grateful to the many people who have contributed in one way or another to the research and production of this book, above all to the families of the Malpai Group itself: the Glenns, McDonalds, Hadleys, Millers, Austins, Winklers, Rooses, Kimbles, Kimbros, Krentzes, Elbrocks, Magoffins, Walters, and Woodlings. Many cooperators in academia, government, and non-governmental organizations have also been extraordinarily helpful and supportive: Larry Allen, Ron Bemis, Ben and Crystal Brown, Jim Brown, Kelly Cash, John Cook, Charles Curtin, Carl Edminster, Don Decker, Gerry Gottfried, Harry Greene, Dave Harlow, Rick and Heather Knight, Rich Kvale, Bill Lehman, Gary Meffe, Curt Meine, Bill Radke, Ray Turner, and Peter Warren. My debt of gratitude to Kris Havstad far exceeds the long-term plan project, which he and the USDA-Agricultural Research Service-Jornada Experimental Range supported in conjunction with a post-doctoral research fellowship. Ben Brown, Seth Hadley, and Jennifer Medina of the Animas Foundation helped me navigate the files of the Gray Ranch; Wendy Glenn, Mary McDonald, and Carrie Krentz did the same in the Malpai office, as did Peter Warren at The Nature Conservancy's Tucson office. Ron Bemis and Don Decker provided time, expertise, and information from the Natural Resources Conservation Service; Paula Medlock assisted me with Forest Service files in the Supervisor's Office of the Coronado National Forest. Darin Jensen, Don Bain, and their interns here at the Berkeley Department of Geography produced the maps. Many colleagues and friends have generously shared thoughts and advice: Guy McPherson, George Ruyle, Dan Robinett, Lynn Huntsinger, Nancy Peluso, Aaron Bobrow-Strain, Jake Kosek, Julie Guthmann, Wendy Wolford, Geoff Mann, Joe Bryan, Ben Gardner, Scott Prudham, and James McCarthy. Jay Dusard, Bill Radke, Warner Glenn, Raymond Harris, and Ross Humphreys were kind enough to contribute photographs, and Jay Dusard also coined the term "working wilderness," which I have borrowed for my title. I am grateful to Ross and Susan Humphreys for friendship, enthusiasm, impromptu childcare, and above all patience with my prolonged effort to complete the manuscript. The same holds, two-fold, for my wife, Lucia, and our children, Henry and Lila. My thanks to all, and to anyone I've inadvertently forgotten to name. I alone am responsible for the final product.

FOLLOWING PAGES: Donnie Kimble checking the herd on his family's ranch, which extends up into the Peloncillo Mountains behind him. In 2001 Kimble sold a conservation easement on the ranch's private land to the Malpai Group.

THE WESTERN RANGE AND THE NEW WEST

The interior West is booming. The population of the eight intermountain states—Arizona, New Mexico, Utah, Nevada, Colorado, Wyoming, Idaho, and Montana—grew three times faster than the rest of the country in the 1990s. Nevada and Arizona are the nation's fastest-growing states, and the fastest-growing counties surround Phoenix and Las Vegas. The West has known booms before—most of them followed by busts. But this boom is apparently different. No longer is the region's economic activity tied closely to natural resource extraction and agriculture, as in the past. Mining, farming, ranching, and timber production are now rather modest parts of the West's economy, and especially of its growth. Nowadays there is a more diversified economy featuring tourism, technology, industry, and professional services. Federal agencies and contractors provide large numbers of reliable jobs, and a steady inflow of newcomers contributes to ongoing growth

across the economy. This boom will continue—consider the baby boomers soon to retire, after all. This booming West is new—the New West.

Although concentrated in the cities, the New West boom has rippled outward and now affects even remote rural areas. The amount of developed land is growing two or three times faster than the population. In Arizona, over 300,000 acres of farm and rangeland was developed *per year* from 1964 to 1997; Montana developed almost 200,000 acres per year, and Colorado, 154,000 acres per year. Approximately 40 million acres of farm and ranch land have gone out of agricultural production in the past forty years. There are still plenty of rural areas that aren't booming, where landscapes are dotted with abandoned farm fields, mobile homes, and For Sale signs. But even in those places, the value of real

estate is not declining. Nationally, more people are moving to rural areas than from them, for the first time since the Depression. Rural residential development—where parcels average ten to forty acres in size—is the nation's fastest growing type of land use since 1950, and now covers almost 25 percent of the continental U.S.

The conversion of open lands to suburbs and exurbs has alarmed Westerners of all stripes: urban and rural residents, landowners and environmentalists alike. But in some quarters the alarm is tempered by the fact that so much of the West is public land. The federal government owns 88 percent of Nevada, 42 percent of Arizona, 39 percent of Colorado, and 36 percent of New Mexico. With large state and tribal land holdings, Arizona is less than 18 percent private land, New Mexico less than 43 percent. The national parks and forests, wildlife refuges, Indian reservations, and even military ranges provide a reassuring sense that the West's great open spaces are protected from real estate development. Indeed, for some the New West ushers in not only a new prosperity but also a cleansed environmental conscience. After all, everyone knows the Old West pillaged the land. Farming uses so much water, and without grazing and timber cutting on the public lands, they argue, the New West may even be a net gain for the environment. In the New West, a quality environment will become an economic asset for "non-consumptive" activities: recreation, tourism, birdwatching, nature appreciation. Economy and ecology will finally align in a "new economy of nature."

At stake in this transformation is America's most legendary and contested landscape: the West's vast open rangelands, "beyond the 100th meridian," where average annual precipitation is less than twenty inches and dry farming is unreliable or impossible. The West's legends and conflicts are rooted in ranching, the dominant land use on some 485 million acres of federal, state, and private lands. For one hundred years, these lands have been used, managed, and governed under a system of institutions, practices, and ideas known as the Western Range. The system depended on several assumptions about how the range worked, what made it valuable, and how it related to the larger economy and society. In the New West these assumptions no longer hold, and the Western Range is falling apart as a result.

How does the Western Range figure into the New West? Should its disintegration be mourned, or celebrated? Can portions of it be retained and retooled to meet new circumstances? The Malpai Borderlands Group presents a set of answers to these questions for one piece of the West. How relevant its answers are to other settings remains to be seen. But the questions apply to the West as a whole.

THE ORIGINS OF THE WESTERN RANGE

The blueprint for the Western Range was produced in 1905 by President Roosevelt's Public Lands Commission.

Throughout the West at that time, and especially in the Southwest, rangelands were in desperate shape. Livestock had flooded into the region during the Cattle Boom of the 1870s and 1880s—the paradigmatic case of the "tragedy of the commons"—taking advantage of free and open land blanketed with grass. Under the nation's homesteading laws, settlers had been able to secure only small areas—less than a square mile—for private ownership. They had chosen sites endowed with water and fertile land, while everything in between had remained open to anyone who wished to use it. The result was disastrous overgrazing. In 1898, H. L. Bentley, one of the first government range researchers, described the boom's origins this way:

> Every man was seized with the desire to make the most that was possible out of his opportunities while they lasted. He reasoned that there was more grass than his own cows could possibly eat. There was plenty of stock water for five times as many cows as were now on the range. There was no rent to pay, and not much in the way of taxes, and while these conditions lasted every stockman thought it well to avail himself of them. Therefore all bought cows to the full extent of their credit on a rising market and at high rates of interest.

Livestock had perished in huge numbers during blizzards on the Great Plains in the 1880s, and again during Southwestern droughts in the 1890s. Cattle bones had been gathered into towering piles next to railheads for shipment to fertilizer plants. Plans for big dams and irrigation works, envisioned under the Newlands Act of 1902, appeared threatened by extreme, widespread erosion. Earlier attempts to reform the laws affecting rangelands had foundered on political shoals, but after the turn of the century no one any longer disputed the need for change.

The Commission's report, based on two years of public hearings and research, opened with a simple statement regarding the West's rangelands: "They are, and probably always will be, of chief value for grazing." Half fact and half prediction, this judgment underpinned everything else the Commission recommended, in particular the system of grazing allotments and permits that was instituted on national forests from that year forward. At the time, livestock production was the only livelihood available across most of the arid and semiarid West, and private lands were typically too small to support a household. The Western Range was intended to give producers secure access to enough land to make a living, thereby bringing about "the largest permanent occupation of the country by actual settlers and home seekers." Twenty-nine years later, under the Taylor Grazing Act, the same basic system was extended to the rest of the West's unclaimed federal rangelands—today's Bureau of Land Management lands.

The ramifications of the Western Range persist to this day. The Taylor Act terminated homesteading in the Lower 48 states, freezing in place the landownership patterns of the time, which have changed only slightly since then: private lands near natural waters and floodplains, where homesteaders managed to carve out a living long enough to perfect title; national forests at higher elevations; state lands, national parks, and Indian reservations scattered here and there; BLM lands everywhere else. The Western Range system also assigned carrying capacities—known as stocking rates, permitted numbers, or preferences—to each public land grazing allotment, figures that were destined to become the focus of conflicts

between ranchers, agencies, and environmentalists for decades to follow. (The idea of carrying capacities, and the science behind them, will be examined more closely in Chapter 3.) In these and other ways, the Western Range set the terms for today's debates, not only on the landscape but also in law, science, and the public mind.

The contradiction between the New West and the Western Range is most conspicuous in the predictive half of the Commission's opening judgment: the fatefully erroneous phrase "and probably always will be." If one measures value by market prices—as the Commission did—then today, the "chief value" of Western rangelands is no longer grazing. A recent study in New Mexico concluded that only 16 percent of the sales price of ranches could be attributed to their agricultural productivity. The other 84 percent was "amenity values": scenery, open

Warner Glenn exercising his hounds on the Malpai Ranch, San Bernardino Valley.

space, climate, wildlife, and so forth. In all but the most isolated settings, the highest-value use of the federal lands is recreation, while that of the private lands is real estate development. The two land types are still economically linked—inasmuch as proximity to public land raises the value of private home sites—but in general, livelihoods are no longer dependent on the land's ecology. In the New West, people want to live on the range, and they will pay handsomely for natural amenities, but they don't need to make their living from it. Had the Commission done its work a century later, the Western Range would have looked completely different.

The central premise of the Western Range, then, was that without foreseeable alternative land uses, the value of ranches would always be a function of their productivity for livestock. Provided with secure tenure to enough grazing land to make a living, the ranchers' self-interest would therefore align with the public's interest in healthy rangelands. The New West's real estate market has pulled the rug out from under this argument, but before about 1970 it was an eminently sound proposition. Yet the Western Range, by most accounts, was at best only a moderate success. Generally speaking, range conditions are better now than in 1905, but not as good as they were in 1870. Particularly in drier regions such as the Southwest, large areas of range have shifted from grass dominance to shrubbier conditions, despite declining numbers of livestock. So what went wrong?

THE ORIGINS OF MUTUAL DISTRUST

For more than fifty years, critics of ranching and the Western Range have aimed their attacks at the motives and incentives of ranchers, accusing them of putting self-interest ahead of the public good. Unsatisfactory ecological conditions have served as evidence for this, but the accusation originated on purely political terrain. By installing federal land management agencies as permanent features of the region's landscape and economy, the Western Range ensured that politics would be different there, and more difficult, than elsewhere in the U.S. Efforts were made to provide local communities, and especially permittees, a strong voice in the administration of Forest Service and BLM grazing lands. But tensions always persisted, and livestock associations and Western political leaders repeatedly called for devolution of federal lands downward—to the states, the counties, or to private ownership. It was these demands that confirmed the critics' conviction that ranchers could not be trusted.

One such proposal reached Congress shortly after World War II, provoking a famous series of rebukes by Bernard DeVoto in the pages of *Harper's*. "Nothing in history suggests that the states are adequate to protect their own resources, or even want to, or to suggest that cattlemen and sheepmen are capable of regulating themselves even for their own benefit, still less the public's," DeVoto wrote witheringly. "Cattlemen and sheepmen, I repeat, want to shovel most of the West into its rivers." DeVoto inverted the mythology of ranching expressed in Western movies and literature, which was then at its height: far from embodiments of frontier valor, ranchers were cast as greedy and venal despoilers of the public trust.

In its basic terms and arguments, the so-called "rangeland conflict" has scarcely changed since DeVoto wrote. The Sagebrush Rebellion of the 1980s made basically the same demand as in 1947, and it was met with basically the same response. In seeking to end federal involvement in their livelihood, the ranching community was perceived as revealing their "real" motivations, which appeared not only selfish but also anti- environmental. Poor range conditions served to ratify the point. Since then, the fundamental intent of the Western Range—to enable private ranchers to make a living from public lands—has come to be viewed by many environmentalists as intrinsically contrary to conservation. Through legislation and lawsuits, they have pressed to curtail or eliminate livestock grazing on federal lands. Proposals for sweeping reform at the federal level have repeatedly been stymied by organized opposition from ranchers, just as ranchers' proposals for devolution of federal lands have been blocked by environmentalists. But the critics of ranching have won many smaller, more incremental or symbolic victories, especially in the courts, and as ranches convert to subdivisions across the West it is easy to conclude that ranching is on its way out.

A more recent variation on DeVoto's argument turns on the question of subsidies. Because grazing fees on public lands are lower than those on private rangelands, Western ranchers are likened to "welfare mothers" dependent on public handouts. The argument is curious in numerous ways. There are some good reasons that private lands fetch higher rates: they tend to be more productive, for one thing, and more services are typically provided. It is also odd to hear environmentalists appealing to free-market principles, given their staunch defense of government intervention in so many realms and of public land ownership in the West in particular. Wasn't it the free market that drove the Cattle Boom in the first place? Moreover, virtually every major segment of American agriculture is subsidized by government; ranching's share of the federal largesse is relatively meager.

There is also a basic inconsistency in the selfishness argument. Western ranching is generally a poor investment, and has been for nearly forty years. Economists consider ranchers "irrational" because they persist in an occupation that consistently yields sub-market, and sometimes negative, returns. It is quite likely, in fact, that ranchers subsidize ranching more than the public does. According to a recent, large study, just over 50 percent of ranches with federal grazing permits can be classified as "hobby ranches," meaning that their owners derive half or more of their income from non-ranch sources.

Considering the opportunity costs forgone by not selling their lands into development, the private subsidy likely dwarfs the public one. In short, if money alone were what motivates ranchers, they would long ago have gotten out of the business altogether.

In retrospect, the ranchers' calls for devolution were strategically disastrous: they succeeded only in rallying opposition around the idea that ranchers were damaging public grazing lands on purpose, in pursuit of private gain. Once this premise was established, the debate could hardly avoid solidifying into an us-versus-them contest of personal attacks and mutual distrust. This didn't necessarily have to be the case. Excessive grazing did occur under the Western Range, not everywhere and not all the time, but often enough to result in certain kinds of degradation. Stocking rates have fallen steadily on most allotments, not only because agencies demanded it but also because the amount of forage available has declined over time. But poor results do not prove malign intent—why would ranchers "want to shovel most of the West into its rivers" when both their incomes and the value of their ranches depended on good range conditions? The fact that ranchers wanted to devolve federal lands to state or county control doesn't necessarily prove anything about their environmental values.

What if the problems of the Western Range were a function of flawed policies and inadequate knowledge, rather than the motives and incentives of ranchers? What if everyone involved—ranchers, agencies, even environmentalists—was working with a poor model of how rangelands worked and how to take care of them for the long term? What if better knowledge and practices have only emerged recently, at just the time when rising real estate values have rendered ranching "irrational"? Based on historical records and the latest research in rangeland

Turkey Creek in the Chiricahua Mountains, where Joe and Valer Austin have installed small rock dams to combat erosion. The Malpai Group has launched similar projects, inspired in part by the Austins, in the San Bernardino Valley.

ecology, one can make a strong argument that this indeed was the case, especially in the Southwest. The details of the argument will emerge in the chapters that follow. In any event, more than fifty years of acrimony—of actively assailing each other's motives and integrity—weigh heavily on both sides of the struggle over the Western Range. Distrust has become an obstacle in its own right, one that new knowledge alone can only begin to overcome.

It seems intuitive: if the Old West damaged the land, then the land will recover when the Old West goes away.

A century of battles over stocking rates has reinforced the idea that degradation is always caused by too many livestock and that fewer animals necessarily equals healthier land. But this intuition—deeply ingrained in our culture and, until recently, shared by the science of ecology—is in fact mistaken. Drier rangelands in particular, such as those of the Great Basin and the Southwest, will not heal themselves upon removal of livestock, any more than an open pit mine will fill itself back in when the bulldozers and dump trucks leave. Strange as it may sound, the very land use that has attended so much damage to the Western Range—livestock ranching—now may be the key to its future conservation. Restoring rangelands to some "pristine" past condition is an impossible fantasy, a product (or a cause?) of outdated ecological theories. But remediation—mitigating past damage and working toward conditions that are better for wildlife and watersheds as well as livestock—is a realistic goal. Ranchers have a direct stake in realizing this goal, especially if they do not want to see their lands turned into homesites.

The Western Range is broken, but the polarized politics of "the rangeland conflict," by pitting ranchers against environmentalists in a kind of holy war, have made wholesale reform unattainable. Instead, innovations have had to emerge from the grass roots, poking up through layers of indifference, habit, and bureaucracy. The stories of these seedling efforts have scarcely been told, let alone collected and evaluated. This is the story of one such grassroots effort, one that has survived and grown for more than a decade. The Malpai Borderlands Group has drawn much of its energy from the deep roots of ranching in the Old West, but it has candidly accepted that new sources and patterns of sustenance must be found, and found quickly. It has reached rich common ground among scientists and some environmental groups, who share a commitment to keeping a large and diverse piece of southern Arizona and New Mexico open and wild. Together, they have redefined the relationship of ranching to government agencies, ecological values, and economic opportunities.

Imagine the Western Range as an enormous puzzle whose pieces have not only come apart but changed their shapes as well. They cannot be put back together according to the old picture, and the easiest course of action is simply to leave it in pieces: five acres here, ten acres there, forty acres someplace else. It is in such sizes, after all, that the pieces marked "private land" find their highest price. The Malpai Group has chosen to look at all the pieces in a 1,250-square-mile part of the puzzle and insist that they can be one whole again. The pieces seem countless—private land, state land, federal land, cattle, water, people, grasses, shrubs, trees, endangered species, invasive species, fire, drought, soils, erosion, money, history, science…on and on and on. Each one requires careful study, but only makes full sense as part of an infinitely complex whole.

The Malpai Group remains many years away from completing this new picture, but they are further along than anyone else. The edges are nearly whole, and large parts of the interior are in place. The outlines of a New Western Range are coming into focus. The picture in the Borderlands is unique: no place else will look exactly like it. But Malpai's progress alone is noteworthy, and its story may help inspire and guide the many other people who share their conviction that the blessings of the West depend on the picture as a whole, no matter how tempting it is to dwell on the pieces. Passing from Old West to New cannot but be a messy process in some degree. But the new boosters and the swelling ranks of New Westerners err in dismissing the Western Range as an irrelevant anachronism or a disgraceful inheritance. Nature will not redeem past sins for free, and sacrificing the Old West on the altar of the New is false propitiation.

As you know, over the past thirty-two years we have lived, worked, and raised a family here in the borderlands. Our great grandparents arrived in the 1880s, less than twenty years after the Civil War and long before the floodgates of the modern world opened, and began to change so many of the beautiful lands in the U.S. We are blessed to live in a place that has remained much as it was when our ancestors first saw it. And like them, we've always felt in our bones the specialness of this country, and the ranching way of life. Every year that passes we feel more keenly than ever that it is our duty to safeguard these treasures. Over time, we have worked with neighbors to solve the many problems that faced us as rural ranchers. In recent years, though, we have been confronted by a range of new forces undermining both our way of life and the health of our lands, forces that seemed beyond our control.

—FROM A LETTER TO NEIGHBORS
BY WENDY AND WARNER GLENN, 1994

CHAPTER 1

CRISIS, CONSENSUS, AND CONSERVATION

The Geronimo Trail fire provided the spark that ignited the Malpai Borderlands Group, but it cannot explain what came before or after: the development of the fuels or the flames' subsequent spread, so to speak. From a larger perspective, there is no single person or event from which the group sprang and no simple way to explain it. It arose from a complex of intersecting crises, some local and some regional or national in scale, and its success is attributable to the combined efforts of many very different people. Along the way, a series of events occurred that in retrospect appears to have been critical in arriving at the present. Without any one of these people and events, things might have gone differently. One cannot tell the story without appearing to privilege one or another part of the whole, if only by the order of introduction. But at every step, it was the combination of people and events that mattered. Perhaps most important were the relationships that developed along the

way, providing the confidence and the capacity to respond to events in new ways. No one could have done what the Malpai Group has done—no one would have even tried—without other people making the leap alongside them. "Malpai will never do anything *to* someone—we will only do something *with* them, at their invitation." This credo has guided the group from its inception, expressing and reflecting the fundamental priority given to voluntary cooperation. No matter how important certain individuals or institutions have been, the strength of the group has come from the community of people acting together. What community means, exactly, is a question that runs throughout the chapters of this book.

THE LANDSCAPE

The Malpai Borderlands Group defines its primary planning area as bounded to the south by Mexico, to the west and north by Arizona Highway 80 and New Mexico Highway 9, and to the east by the edge of the Gray Ranch (see Map 1, page 35). It encompasses the Animas Mountains on the Continental Divide, most of the Peloncillo Mountains, which straddle the Arizona-New Mexico border, and the upper portions of the San Bernardino, San Simon, and Animas valleys. It is high and dry country. The valley bottoms lie between 4,000 and 5,000 feet above sea level and receive, on average, about twelve inches of moisture per year. Atop the mountains, at 7,000 to 8,500 feet, precipitation averages rise to as much as twenty inches per year. These averages, however, disguise wide variation from month to month and year to year. A single storm may drop four inches, whereas in the worst droughts that much rain may not fall in twelve months. The heat, wind, and aridity can evaporate one hundred inches of water in a year—nearly ten times the amount that falls from the sky.

The Malpai Group's boundaries reflect both its mission and the current state of land use in the area. The pressures of subdivision and residential real estate development are highest where paved roads provide ready access to the outside world's services and amenities. The city of Douglas (population 15,000) lies just off the southwestern tip of the planning area, face to face across the border with Agua Prieta, Sonora (estimated population 150,000); two small towns, Rodeo and Animas, New Mexico, are located along the highways that define its northern edge. Apart from a nineteen-mile stretch of county highway south of Animas, though, no paved roads penetrate the interior of the planning area, where ranches dominate and the landscape is unfragmented except for fences and dirt or gravel roads. Livestock are raised on all but two properties: the San Bernardino National Wildlife Refuge and a small research ranch tucked up in the Peloncillos. Several large ranches straddle the northwest side of the triangle, running up into the Chiricahua Mountains, and for this reason there is a "secondary planning area" that takes in those mountains. But this also introduces the complication of subdivided lands along the highway outside Douglas and more recently around Rodeo.

Landownership may be the most important and difficult factor in the Malpai Group's efforts to conserve and enhance this landscape. Private ranchers own slightly less than three-fifths of the land in the primary planning area. The states of Arizona and New Mexico own almost a quarter, and federal agencies own the rest (slightly less than one-fifth). These figures are skewed by the enormous Gray Ranch, whose 272,000 acres of private land are anomalous. Without the Gray, the Borderlands are fairly typical of ranch lands in the Southwest: a roughly equal mix of private (41 percent), state (34 percent) and federal (25 percent) ownerships. The federal land is further divided into national forest, BLM, and national wildlife refuge property. Ecologically, of course, all these types of land are interconnected and interdependent. But each has its own legal, political, and economic attributes and constraints.

It is critical to understand that the different types of ownership are not randomly distributed across the landscape. The earliest private land—now the national wildlife refuge—dates to the Spanish Colonial period, when Ignacio Pérez founded the San Bernardino Ranch around a complex of springs and streams straddling today's international border. The water was abundant and pure, and the adjacent floodplain was carpeted with giant sacaton, a prolific grass well suited to livestock. The soils there, formed by periodic deposition of fine flood-borne sediments, were far more productive than anything found in the surrounding hills and mountains. Pérez cleared fields from the floodplain and planted corn, beans, squash, and fruit trees. In 1820, he petitioned the Crown for 73,240 acres, and two years later he acquired the land at auction from the newly independent Mexican state. In the 1830s, however, Apache unrest forced him to abandon the ranch. His cattle went feral, and the land grant hung in legal limbo for nearly fifty years following the Gadsden Purchase of 1854, which brought present-day southern Arizona into the U.S. Ultimately, the courts confirmed title to 2,383 acres in favor of former Texas Ranger John Slaughter. The rest of the original grant lies in Mexico, where it is still a private ranch known as Rancho San Bernardino. Most of the U.S. portion was bought by the Fish and Wildlife Service in 1982 to protect rare native fish.

The San Bernardino was endowed with more water than any other location in the Borderlands, but the same basic principle persisted through the homestead period: private land was carved out where surface water could be found. Any settler aspiring to make a living from the land immediately recognized that water was the key resource, whether for crops or livestock. The

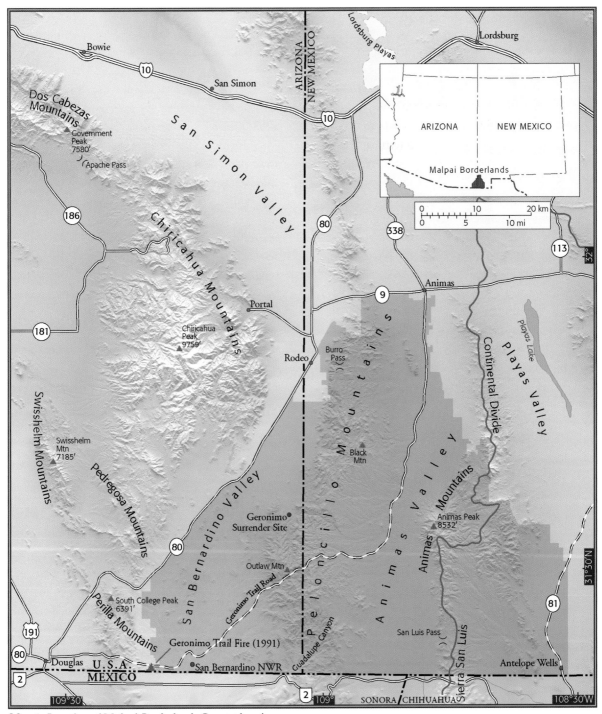

Map 1: Location of Malpai Borderlands Group planning area

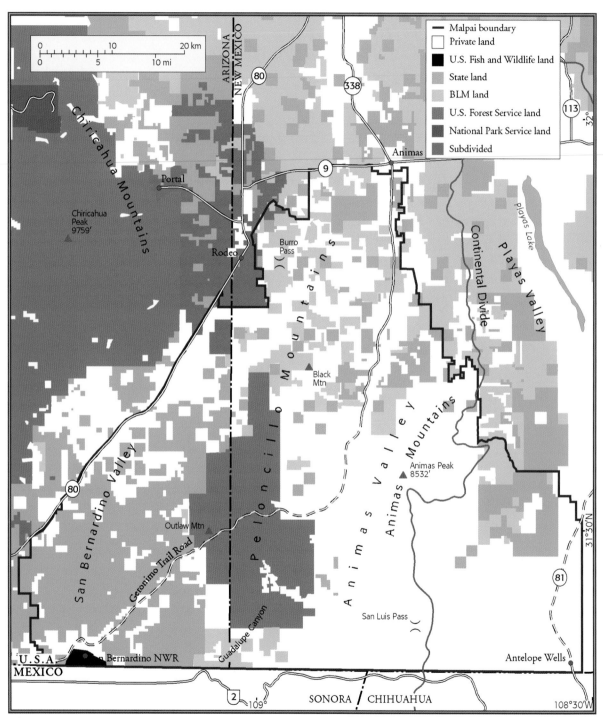

Map 2: Landownership in the Malpai Borderlands Group planning area

Homestead Act and its successor laws permitted settlers to claim only limited areas of private land—between 160 and 640 acres—based on the assumption that crop agriculture would form the backbone of the economy. Only wealthier "settlers" such as George Hearst and his partners (and to a lesser extent John Slaughter) could afford to circumvent the statutes by enlisting others to file claims on waterless land—this is how the anomalous Gray Ranch came into being in the last two decades of the nineteenth century. Actual homesteaders could only hope to own a few fields and pastures and to leverage a measure of control over the surrounding range by monopolizing the water. As windmills and wells became more common around 1900, homesteaders became less dependent on natural surface waters, but they continued to concentrate along washes and floodplains where groundwater was shallow.

Gradually the land not homesteaded passed into various kinds of public administration. The higher parts of the Peloncillo and Animas Mountains became forest reserves in 1906 and later were consolidated into the Coronado National Forest. After Arizona and New Mexico attained statehood in 1912, portions of the valleys became state trust lands. What remained—generally the least productive lands—remained open for homesteading until the Taylor Grazing Act of 1934 and are now administered by the Bureau of Land Management. All of these lands were divided into large pieces, fenced, and leased to the owners of nearby private parcels; together, the leased allotments and the old homesteads formed viable ranch units. The Gray Ranch, again, was an exception to this pattern. In 1952, the Forest Service traded away its holdings in the Animas Mountains to the owners of the Gray, creating the only privately owned mountain range in the region.

This historical process has produced a legacy of enormous ecological consequence. In general, the private land in the Borderlands, as in the West as a whole, lies along streams and rivers or around springs and seeps. It tends to be located where the soils are richest and where floodwaters deposit the most rainfall in the form of run-off. This concentration of nutrients and moisture makes the private lands more biologically productive than the surrounding uplands and mountains. Thus, even where private lands are a small part of the landscape, what happens there has a disproportionate impact on the ecosystem and its inhabitants, particularly wildlife. The future of these ecosystems thus depends largely on the use and management of private lands.

DRUM HADLEY

Ranchers sometimes joke that ranching is a genetic defect—something you inherit and can't be rid of, no matter how you try. The humor relates indirectly to their obsession with the genetics of their cattle and their ongoing struggles to cull underperforming animals from their herds. Directly, it draws on the contradictory experiences of running a ranch: exasperating, exhausting, unpredictable, an emotional and financial roller coaster, yet irresistibly fulfilling and beautiful. It is a way of expressing the sentiment that they love it in part because there is so much to hate about it—the toil and frustration somehow contribute to the love, not unlike raising children.

Telling the joke also helps bridge the gap between the two ways people can get into ranching, by birth or by purchase, and this is perhaps where the real humor lies. Very few people get rich from livestock ranching, but many rich people have become ranchers, sinking significant wealth from other sources into a livelihood that has long been economically irrational. They could make better money in the stock market, or even in treasury notes. Yet since its beginnings in the second half of the nineteenth century, the Western ranching community has been a blend of people born into it—economically marginal and sporadically culled by debt, drought, and the market—and people of substantial wealth who ranch because they love it and who can afford to lose money in the cattle business. The joke is often told in the company of both types, and it helps affirm their common predicament and efface their other disparities. If ranching is a defective gene, dominant among those born into it, the rich apparently have it in its recessive form. The Malpai Group includes both types, and if they couldn't joke about it, they probably wouldn't be able to work together effectively.

Drummond Hadley is a supreme example of the second type of rancher. Born into the Anheuser-Busch fortune, Drum came to the Southwest to attend the University of Arizona. He studied English and poetry, and through family connections befriended Gary Snyder and other luminaries of 1960s alternative culture. But the rugged Southwestern landscape drew him more strongly than the protest movement. In 1971 or thereabouts, he pushed his saddle through the border fence and walked to the Rancho San Bernardino to find work as a *vaquero*, a cowboy. It was ancient work, some three hundred years old in northern Mexico and centuries older at its origins in Spain. It combined culture and landscape, work and play, tools and techniques, songs and stories. For two years it absorbed Drum and Drum absorbed it. He came back, just barely, in 1973 when he bought the Guadalupe Canyon Ranch along the international border in the southern Peloncillo Mountains.

Drum Hadley training his border collie.

In the 1970s and 80s, Drum and his wife, Diana, raised their children and managed the ranch and gradually became trusted members of the local community despite Drum's utterly un-rancher-like idiosyncrasies and dispositions. Poet, cowboy, iconoclast, and visionary, he cultivated radical ideas about the land and an unusually broad circle of friends. Guadalupe Canyon became a cross between a laboratory and a salon. Drum managed his cattle to restore Guadalupe Creek by keeping them out of the riparian corridor during the summer, when young trees could establish. He rearranged his fences to make pastures reflect the landscape's topography instead of cadastral section lines. In late-night gatherings, he honed his ideas in conversations with ranchers, writers, environmentalists, and scientists. He continued to work and socialize with old-timers on both sides of the international border, collecting their stories and distilling them into poems. Drum credits one old cowboy in particular, Walter Ramsey, with teaching him that the range had previously had more grass and fewer shrubs. From scientists, Drum learned that shrub encroachment was at least partially due to the absence of fires since the 1890s, and he became an ardent advocate of bringing fire back.

There is a long list of birds and plants that are fairly common in Arizona but found nowhere else in New Mexico except Guadalupe Canyon. Like those species, Drum refuses all human boundaries. The whole Malpai Borderlands, he points out, was until fairly recently "a horseback culture," in which the international border was more or less irrelevant. Someone looking for something—flour, a spare part, a dinner companion—was as likely to ride across the line as they were to go into town by car. This borderless equestrianism ended in the 1970s, according to Drum, with the building of Mexico Highway 2, which runs east from Agua Prieta to Janos, Chihuahua. By U.S. standards it is a small highway—two rather narrow lanes and virtually no shoulders—but it is busy enough to pose a barrier to local, everyday, horseback riders. In their place are outsiders passing through at sixty miles per hour, scarcely noticing the landscape. Drum feels the loss acutely, and preventing it from spreading further into the Malpai Borderlands is a cause that stirs him to poetry, to philanthropy, and occasionally to profanity. Drum is credited as the source of many of the ideas that have raised the Malpai Group to prominence, but the implementation of those ideas has been led by ranchers with still deeper roots in the area. We will meet them in subsequent chapters.

JIM CORBETT AND THE MALPAI AGENDA

In the late 1980s and early 1990s, relations between ranchers and environmentalists had reached new lows. On road signs in rural ranching areas, bumper stickers were appearing that read "Cattle Free by '93"—the slogan of a national campaign to end public lands grazing. Across Arizona and New Mexico, public and private agencies—The Nature Conservancy, the U.S. Fish and Wildlife Service, and the Bureau of Land Management, in particular—were buying ranches and removing the livestock, to the delight of environmentalists and the frustration of ranchers. At livestock association meetings, the "enviros" were routinely called communists or agents of the UN. One Tucson activist published a large book called *The Waste of the West*, which argued that ranching was a vast socio-cultural conspiracy, degrading minds as well as land. Beneath a graphic picture of a decaying carcass, he wrote: "As a warning to stop our ranching-reform efforts, a local stockman shot our dog, skinned it, and dumped it near our house."

Drum Hadley found this atmosphere poisonous and counter-productive, and the Geronimo Trail fire underscored his point. Ranchers and environmentalists alike could see the value of letting it burn, he felt, yet it had been extinguished. This was frustrating, but also humbling for Drum and his neighbors. Clearly they did not have much influence over the Forest Service's decisions regarding fire, and this seemed but one of several realms in which their autonomy was eroding. They took pride in acting together to solve collective problems—in recent years they had organized to bring electricity, telephones, and school bus service to the San Bernardino Valley and the Peloncillo Mountains. But new threats seemed beyond their control: the Forest Service's fire policies, the loss of grasslands to shrubs, the loss of ranchlands to suburban development, and the rising opposition of environmentalists. In Warner and Wendy Glenn's words, "our children could look forward and see they wouldn't be able to make it ranching."

Jim Corbett at work in the San Pedro Valley.

In porch conversations, Drum urged his neighbors to organize, as they had done before, but also to reach out to their critics. He believed ranchers and environmentalists could resolve their differences, or at least they could get along with each other—he had friends in both camps, after all, and his ranch was living testimony to his view that livestock and the environment were not incompatible. As he saw it, the problem was ignorance, born of a lack of communication: ranchers had failed to explain their situation and their way of life to the outside world. To remedy this, Drum invited some environmentalists he knew to meet with some of his neighbors to discuss their goals and their differences. Included were the head of the New Mexico Audubon Society, which had taken an interest in Guadalupe Canyon, as well as activists from Gila, New Mexico. Some of the environmentalists wanted to meet at a "neutral site," but Drum insisted that they gather on a ranch, and the first meeting took place at the Glenns' Malpai Ranch in September of 1991, two months after the Geronimo Trail fire.

One of the regulars at these meetings was Jim Corbett, whose role in the Malpai Group was small but seminal. He came to the area in the 1980s as a leader in the Sanctuary Movement, a network of civic and religious groups who operated a modern-day underground railroad for refugees fleeing the civil wars in El Salvador and Guatemala. Over and over, Corbett walked through the canyons of the southern Peloncillos, tracing paths to the border fence, where he met small groups of refugees and guided them into the U.S. He said little, at peace with his thoughts and the desert nights even while engaged in actions the federal government considered felonious. In a highly publicized trial in 1986, a jury found him not guilty of smuggling aliens—the government's case was weakened by the fact that his voice never appeared on their secretly recorded tapes. He passed away in 2001 on a small farm in Cascabel, in the opposite corner of Cochise County from the Malpai Borderlands.

Drum was a well-heeled cowboy-poet, and Jim was an ascetic pastoralist-philosopher, but they hit it off right away. Both could sympathize with and evoke respect from ranchers and environmentalists. Corbett had studied at Harvard and worked as a farmer, a cowboy, and a goatherd in Arizona and in Mexico. In the late 1980s and the 1990s he had watched his friends and neighbors in the Cascabel area feud bitterly with environmentalists over livestock grazing along the San Pedro River. The Nature Conservancy had purchased a large, legendary ranch called the Muleshoe and removed all the livestock. When the BLM agreed to let the Conservancy retain leasehold without grazing, a neighboring rancher sued. Many locals' feelings toward the Conservancy, the federal government, and environmentalists are to this day colored by the battles of that period.

The idea of a dialogue between ranchers and environmentalists may well have been Jim's. As a Quaker, he found the animosity regrettable and the tactics highhanded. Partially in response, in 1988 he had helped found the Saguaro-Juniper Association, a consensus-based organization dedicated to an area of land located between the San Pedro and the Muleshoe. Saguaro-Juniper owns and leases land and grazes livestock under a covenant, in both the real estate and the religious senses of the word. The covenant includes a "bill of rights for the land": to be free from human-accelerated erosion, to evolve without human scarring or domination, and not to have its constituent elements treated as "mere commodities." If this sounds like conventional wilderness protection, it's not. Corbett believed that human communities are part of the natural world, not outside of it, and that striving for sustainable coexistence with nature is both a spiritual and a practical calling. In 1991 he published *Goatwalking: A Guide to Wildland Living, a Quest for the Peaceable Kingdom*. It is a meditation on living in the desert, on human spirituality, and on the role that livestock can play in both. It begins this way:

Two milk goats can provide all the nutrients a human being needs, with the exception of vitamin C and a few common trace elements. Learn the relevant details about range-goat husbandry and something about edible plants, and with a couple of milk goats you can feed yourself in most wildlands, even in deserts.

Civilized human beings don't fit into untamed communities of plants and animals, as members of the community. Instead of adapting to wildlands, we tame them. The goat-human partnership can fit in, which opens a way for errantry. Goatwalking is errantry that takes the goat-human partnership's adaptation to wildlands as its point of departure.

Errantry is primarily concerned with communion, which in our age focuses on the harmonious adaptation of human civilization to life on earth. The first, decisive step into errantry is to become untamed, at home in wildlands. To be at home in wildlands, one must accept and share life as a gift that is unearned and unowned. When we cease to work at taming the Creation and learn to accept life as a gift, a way opens for us to become active participants in an ancient exodus out of idolatry and bondage—a pilgrimage that continues to be conceived and born in wilderness.

Corbett's philosophy turns the conventional arguments about ranching and conservation inside out. Instead of being radically opposed, livestock and wilderness become mutually reinforcing, even mutually dependent. Goats make it possible for a person to live in wilderness, and living in wilderness makes it possible to achieve—or at least glimpse—communion with nature and spirit. Valuing nature in its own right and becoming at home in wildlands are thus seen as goals *made possible* by livestock, in both a human-evolutionary sense and in an individual's practical life.

Through the fall of 1991 and the first half of 1992, Drum and Jim and a growing assortment of others continued to meet periodically. Ray Turner, an ecologist, Saguaro-Juniper member, and Drum's father-in-law, joined them and became a regular, providing a relatively independent scientific voice. They began to call themselves the Malpai discussion group, after the Glenns' ranch, although the meetings rotated among ranches in the area. In Quaker fashion, Jim pressed for consensus: focus on identifying where all parties could agree, and agree to disagree on other things. On the issue of livestock grazing, consensus was elusive, but common ground emerged on two related topics: everyone preferred the land open and undeveloped, and everyone was concerned about the replacement of grasses by shrubs. Even those who disliked livestock agreed that ranches were preferable to subdivisions, at the very least because the grasses needed fire and fire could not be restored where houses dotted the landscape.

The last meeting of the discussion group was held at Drum's ranch in July 1992. From it came the founding document of the Malpai Borderlands Group, anonymously authored by Jim Corbett. "The Malpai Agenda for Grazing in the Sonoran and Chihuahuan Bioregions" began by describing the polarized battle between ranchers and environmentalists. "To reverse this polarization, which is a no-win situation for the land and everyone concerned, the 'Malpai Meeting' proposes that a concerted effort be made to identify the conservational common ground that unites all of us who love the land, then to create programs in which we can work together to implement the values we share." One may love wilderness "as an Eden unspoiled by human sins" or as a specific place where one lives and raises a family, Corbett wrote. These have different roots, but "in both cases 'love' means valuing the land in itself, and this is the foundation for establishing basic rights for native biotic communities." He then restated the covenant ideas of Saguaro-Juniper and *Goatwalking*, contextualized in social and political, rather than theological, terms:

In the Sonoran and Chihuahuan bioregions and most of the arid West, ranching is now the only livelihood that is based on human adaptation to wild biotic communities. Few dispute that livestock have done serious damage and continue to do so in some places. Few dispute that yearlong, sedentary grazing will degrade plant communities in arid lands. To continue in this bioregion, livestock grazing must discontinue practices that degrade the land. The real issue is the preservation of the last remnant of the livelihoods based on human adaptation to wildlands—pastoral adaptation that seeks to fit into the untamed biotic community, not to remake the land and replace its natives to fit our civilization.

All who love the land agree that it should not be cashed-in or mined-out and that its health takes precedence over profits. They agree in their opposition to "development" that bulldozes and fractures the land, drains away its waters, and poisons it with wastes. In debates that pit preservation against development, all who know and love a wildland are on the side of its preservation. Conservationists who are ranchers are divided from many other conservationists by their belief that ranching can be stewardship that preserves the health and unreduced diversity of the native biotic community.

Much more is at stake here than the future of a few ranch families. Wildlands teach those for whom they are home an outlook and insights to which others are blind. Some of these lessons take many generations to learn… These lessons come hard, and no society that eradicates or discards those among its members who have acquired this kind of wisdom can mature into a people that is truly at home in its land. How to fit-in responsibly, as supportive members of a native biotic community, is a meaningful question only for those who live by fitting-in somehow.

These paragraphs do not so much resolve the rangeland conflict as transcend it. That ranching must respect and protect the ecological values of the range is granted outright. No environmentalist could ask for a higher standard than "the health and unreduced diversity of the native biotic community." Yet the value to which this standard is linked is not native biodiversity in itself but the physical and spiritual well-being of humanity, and in this connection ranching assumes a role that environmentalism can neither claim nor discredit, no matter how biocentric or altruistic it may purport to be. People must learn to live with the land. "Protected" areas where people are excluded cannot teach this. Consider ranching by comparison to all the other ways people make a living in our society, and no matter how grave its flaws or its historical misdeeds, it stands out for its dependence on native biota and unaltered landscapes. Its lessons and knowledge—its wisdom—thus become crucial for the effort of society as a whole to become "truly at home in its land."

On this basis, the Malpai Agenda proposed three program areas. The first was called simply Common Ground. "If ranchers and anti-grazing conservationists can agree on conservation principles, the resolution of many of their differences would be a matter of verifiable facts. They would then have a common ground for cooperation, study, and joint efforts. Conservationists who disagree about livestock grazing on arid lands but who

Looking west from near the town of the Animas, New Mexico; the Chiricahua Mountains rise in the distance.

agree to seek a resolution of their differences should meet to discover whatever conservation ethic they share." The second, Information and Education, called for more systematic monitoring and research on biotic change in the Sonoran and Chihuahuan bioregions. Such efforts would help ranchers improve their management and provide opportunities for the general public "to learn firsthand on both sides of the border about ranching, range management, and concerns about livestock impacts on native biotic communities."

The final program area, Base-Community Development, articulated a vision of the political institutions necessary to achieve conservation in a landscape of multiple public and private landowners. "Livestock have been most destructive in the Sonoran and Chihuahuan bioregions when the common use of land hasn't been matched by community decision-making. Where community decision-making is undeveloped, everyone may see what needs to be done to save our common heritage of life-supporting soils, waters, native plants, and wildlife, but no one can do anything about it. Where a community agrees about its conservation principles and how to implement them, it can enact its land ethic as the law of its land, formulated in conservation covenants." This would put local landowners in a position of parity with larger institutions. Locals would be "partners rather than patients" in relation to federal agencies and national environmental groups, empowered "to protect their land when outside agencies seek to institute uses and developments that would degrade and damage it."

The goal was the same as in *Goatwalking* and Saguaro-Juniper—harmonious relations both among people and between people and land. Pointing to the San Pedro River, Corbett noted that partnerships with landowners were often undermined by the emphasis placed on land acquisition. Instead, conservation easements should be used to protect landscapes and local livelihoods together. "When such conservation easements are broadened into mutually binding agreements that obligate the federal government, local landowners, and nongovernmental conservation organizations to observe the same rules or practices (regardless of future shifts in federal policies), they become covenants that establish among all parties a genuine partnership in conservation. A viable land ethic is far more likely to be established and to persist by means of voluntary, pluralistic 'private law' of this kind than by political contests, new statutes, federal regulations, and expropriation."

A consensus had been reached among a small group of ranchers and environmentalists regarding ranching and conservation. The Malpai Agenda diagnosed the problem as a political one, and it proposed a solution that combined science with a new, locally driven and more collaborative political approach. It did not specify what should be done, exactly, but rather how things should be done—a process by which to make decisions in pursuit of a viable land ethic. The discussion group had fulfilled its purpose of encouraging dialogue and clarifying issues, and it did not meet again.

FIRE

The Malpai Agenda didn't say a word about fire, and only a handful of local ranchers had participated in its formulation. But fire suppression was the clearest example of the need for greater input from local landowners into government land management policies, and the Geronimo Trail fire illustrated the point vividly. The suppression of that fire, over the objections of the rancher whose land was burning, struck everyone in the local community as egregious. For some it was primarily an ecological issue—the grasses needed fire to compete with the brush. For others, it was a classic example of government waste—why spend money putting out a fire that threatened no one's life or property? For most of a century, the Forest Service had diligently extinguished fires in the area, just as it had in the West as a whole, and no one had objected. Now, however, opinion had changed. The energy and ideas contained in the Malpai Agenda emboldened Drum and the Glenns to speak out, and to do so collectively with their neighbors. Wendy and Warner invited every landowner in the area to meet at the Malpai Ranch.

On March 28, 1993, consensus was reached again, this time among thirty people from nineteen ranches and the refuge. "We, the undersigned, are committed to the development of a fire management plan for the area encompassed by the ranches we represent. We request that the agencies involved coordinate with us in the development of this plan." It was an announcement presented as an invitation: We will develop a fire plan, and we ask that you coordinate with us. They began to assemble a map that showed what each landowner wanted done if a fire broke out: let it burn, decide at the

A prescribed fire on the San Bernardino National Wildlife Refuge.

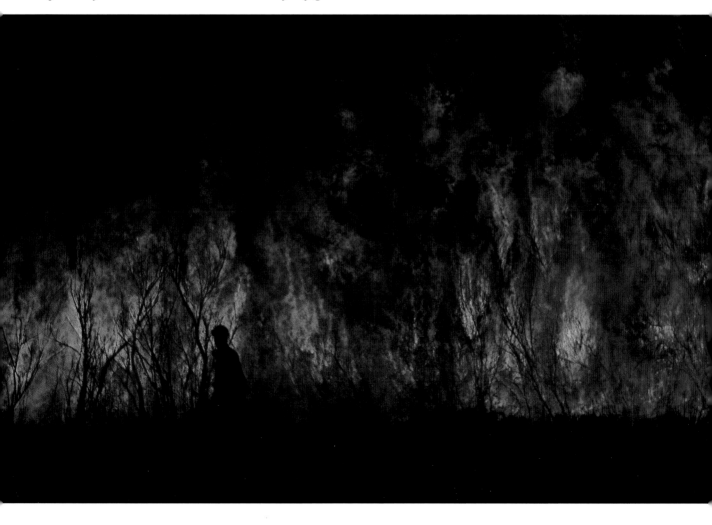

time, or suppress immediately. Each ranch provided a contact name and phone number (telephones were a fairly recent development at that time), which were included in the map legend. They asked Ron Bemis, a range conservationist with the Soil Conservation Service, to help coordinate the effort.

Four weeks later another meeting was held, at the Gray Ranch, with representatives from all of the agencies: the Coronado National Forest, the Arizona and New Mexico offices of the BLM and the Soil Conservation Service, the Arizona and New Mexico State Land departments, the New Mexico State Forester's Office, and two conservation districts. Bill McDonald, Drum Hadley, and the Glenns reiterated the ranchers' desire to see fire returned to the landscape. Ray Turner presented evidence of long-term vegetation change in the borderlands, away from grasses and towards shrubs, and suggested this was due to fire suppression. Guy McPherson, another prominent grassland ecologist, emphasized the importance of hot, summer fires to kill the shrubs: this was the natural fire regime, he said, triggered by monsoon lightning.

Ron Bemis, former Malpai Coordinator for the Natural Resources Conservation Service.

Then, each agency representative spoke. They explained that in both states, fire suppression was the law. Letting a fire burn required a prescription—a careful plan specifying conditions of temperature, wind speed, humidity, and so on—approved ahead of time. The Forest Service was interested in allowing more fires to burn, but it needed coordination across landownership types as well as fire prescriptions. Simply letting naturally ignited fires burn wouldn't be sufficient, they pointed out. Ranchers would need to remove their livestock for a year or two before and after fires, to allow fuels to build up and grasses to recover. Finally, fire had to be a means, not an end in itself: some defined goals were needed to justify all the burning and to measure the effectiveness of a fire plan.

The meeting ran across two days. At the end, consensus was reached for a third time. Agencies' fire control policies would henceforth be "informed and guided by the management goals of the ranchers." In the short term, the fire map would be completed and a protocol developed to coordinate fire response among different agencies in the two states. Over the longer term, a fire-management plan would be developed for the region as a whole, with clear goals and a commitment to large prescribed burns. To advance this agenda, an agreement was drafted and signed committing the agencies to "a coordinated, comprehensive ecosystem management approach" in the area. This would not be limited to fire but would seek "to enhance and restore the use of natural processes in these ecosystems, to improve their renewable resources, to provide for wildlife habitat and productivity of grasslands, and to sustain rural and grazing livelihoods."

——

Three moments of consensus had been attained over the course of eighteen months: first among a small group of ranchers and environmentalists on the subject of ranching, then among all the local landowners on the subject of fire, and finally among landowners and government agencies regarding cooperative management of the area's ecosystems. A core group of people—Drum Hadley, Bill and Mary McDonald, Ray Turner, and Warner and Wendy Glenn—had participated in all three, pulling together an unusual coalition that included all the major "stakeholders" in the area's landscape. Each group had gone on record voicing support for one or more of a set of basic goals and principles: preventing subdivision and residential development, returning fire to the landscape, protecting native flora and fauna, and making decisions cooperatively. These moments of consensus endowed the group with a kind of authority to act in behalf of the landscape they shared.

Consensus rarely comes quickly, and the time spent in all these meetings was considerable. But the effort was rapidly gaining momentum. A year later, in 1994, the Malpai Borderlands Group was formally incorporated as an independent not-for-profit corporation. In name and philosophy, it descended from the discussion group and the Malpai Agenda. It no longer contained ranchers and environmentalists in roughly equal numbers, however. The Malpai Group's by-laws stipulated that one board member would be a scientist and the rest would be local landowners. Environmentalists and agencies would be partners, but private landowners would lead. By this point, however, another event had intervened and caused several of the landowners to withdraw: The Nature Conservancy had bought and sold the Gray Ranch, briefly becoming the area's largest landowner. Instead of simply leaving, moreover, the Conservancy had thrown its support behind the Malpai Group, at the Group's invitation.

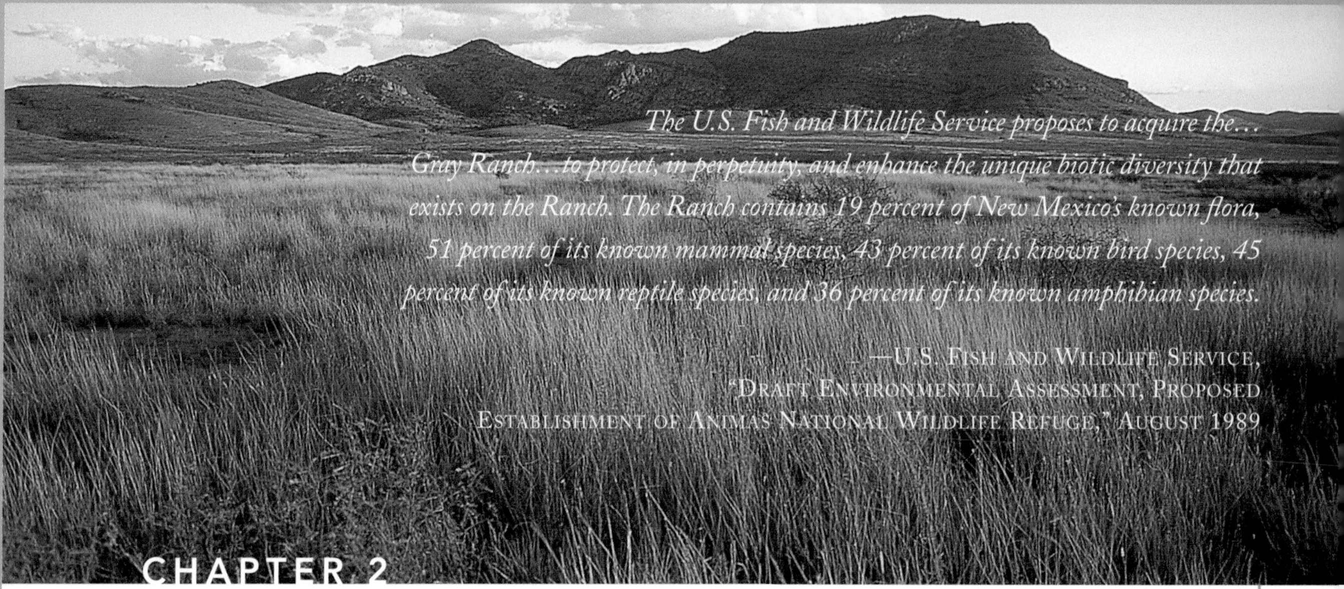

CHAPTER 2

The U.S. Fish and Wildlife Service proposes to acquire the…
Gray Ranch…to protect, in perpetuity, and enhance the unique biotic diversity that
exists on the Ranch. The Ranch contains 19 percent of New Mexico's known flora,
51 percent of its known mammal species, 43 percent of its known bird species, 45
percent of its known reptile species, and 36 percent of its known amphibian species.

—U.S. Fish and Wildlife Service,
"Draft Environmental Assessment, Proposed
Establishment of Animas National Wildlife Refuge," August 1989

Gray Ranch

The minute the ranch is given to the public it will be destroyed.

—Cordelia Cowan, local
rancher, quoted in the *New
York Times*, June 3, 1990

The Gray Ranch sits atop the Borderlands like a crown, the Animas Mountains rising majestically from a golden-green ring of unbroken prairie. Known also (and presently) by its brand, Diamond A, it is superlative in every way: bigger, higher, more visually stunning, more diverse and ecologically intact than its neighbors—indeed, more so than almost any ranch anywhere. In the late 1970s the Gray Ranch was declared the ecosystem most worthy of protection in New Mexico, which is to say that it was the most ecologically significant private land in the state—"private" being understood as the opposite of "protected." In 1983 it changed hands in settlement of a debt and went up for sale, and for more than six years it hung suspended on

the market. At stake in its fate was the future course of the entire area. Who would buy this crown, and what would they do with it? Would it become a national wildlife refuge? A tourist attraction? A billionaire's trophy? A gigantic development? Could it possibly remain a ranch? In January 1990 The Nature Conservancy bought it for $18 million, in what President and CEO John Sawhill called "the largest private land acquisition in conservation history." Its future remained up in the air, however, because the Conservancy didn't intend to keep it. National environmental groups were adamant that the Gray should become a public preserve—that was

what "protected" meant to them. People at local, county, and state levels were equally vehement that it should remain a working, private ranch—from their point of view, that was how its treasures had been "protected" for more than a century already.

The struggle between these diametrically opposed visions of nature on the Gray continued for four years, and at first it was just a coincidence that the Malpai Group was germinating at the same time on the other side of the Peloncillo Mountains. The Conservancy took no part in the Malpai Agenda, and with one exception area ranchers did not participate in negotiations over the Gray. If anything, the local community expected the Conservancy to pursue the same course it had followed a decade earlier, when it had bought the San Bernardino Ranch and then sold it to the U.S. Fish and Wildlife Service to create a national wildlife refuge. They lobbied vigorously to prevent this, and when their efforts succeeded the Conservancy found itself in a bind: unable to afford to keep the Gray but unable to sell it either.

BELOW AND PAGE 53: Repeat photographs of Animas Mountains and Animas Creek, taken 1913 (left) and 1994 (right). The creek runs from right-center of the photos downstream to the lower left, where it meets a tributary that drains the northwest flank of the mountains. Three changes are noteworthy. First, the increased incidence of mesquite trees, particularly along the tributary floodplain but also on the uplands, where the shrub has encroached from lower elevation terrain off-camera to the left. Second, the shift in the location of the creek bed. Third, the emergence of a cottonwood-willow canopy forest along the creek. Many environmentalists insist that grazing must be excluded from such forests to protect the habitat of neo-tropical birds and native aquatic species. Yet in this case and many others, the forests emerged in the presence of livestock grazing, due principally to altered hydrological patterns related to arroyo formation. Evidence assembled by Ray Turner and colleagues (who provided these photos) suggests that there is much more cottonwood-willow riparian forest in the Southwest today than at the time of Anglo settlement.

The Conservancy's predicament appeared entirely distinct from the one that motivated the Malpai Agenda. But the two intersected through Drum Hadley, and the relationships that gradually developed enabled each predicament to help resolve the other. The Gray remained a private ranch with livestock, but in the ownership of a not-for-profit organization called the Animas Foundation, set up by the Hadley family and dedicated to conservation. In working out this arrangement, the Conservancy's lead negotiator, John Cook, came to know and trust the members of the Malpai Group, and they invited him to help pursue the agenda they had formulated on their own. Together, the Malpai Group and the Animas Foundation found a way to bring "private" and "protected" together, not only on the Gray but also on surrounding ranches as well.

ECOLOGY AND HISTORY

The Gray Ranch in 1990 comprised some 321,000 acres—502 square miles—in the "boot heel" of far southwestern New Mexico. It had historically been even larger, and it has expanded in recent years, but its enormous dimensions are the least of its unique qualities. In the upper Animas Valley it contains the largest intact piece of short-grass prairie in the Southwest, a seemingly endless rolling plain of buffalo grass, blue grama, and other native species. Unlike in most of the neighboring valleys, non-native grasses are scarce. Above this plain rise the Animas Mountains, contained almost wholly within the ranch and forming the continental divide from the Mexican border north some twenty-five miles. Due to its location and topography, the Gray is home to organisms that evolved in the Rocky Mountains, the Great Plains, the Chihuahuan Desert, the Sierra Madre, and the Sonoran Desert: more than seven hundred plant species in all, as well as seventy-five different mammals and fifty-two kinds of reptiles and amphibians. And unlike most ranches in the Southwest, the Gray does not depend heavily on state or federal leases. Roughly 87 percent of the ranch is private land, including the Animas Mountains.

The ranch takes its name from its first homesteaders, John and Michael Gray, who perfected their claim in the early 1880s but then quickly sold it to a partnership of wealthy Californians: George Hearst, James Ben Ali Haggin, Lloyd Tevis, and Addison Head. With fortunes from mining, banking, railroads, insurance, and law, the Californians bought up another 150 properties in southwestern New Mexico by 1899, aiming to assemble a ranch property comparable to their

enormous irrigated farm holdings in the San Joaquin Valley. They incorporated the New Mexico ranches as the Victorio Land and Cattle Company, taking the name of the penultimate Apache warrior. By 1905 the company controlled land from the Gray Ranch north and east nearly 150 miles, as well as the 700-square-mile Armendaris Ranch along the Rio Grande in central New Mexico. Early in the twentieth century the Victorio ran perhaps 70,000 cattle across these holdings, although even they probably didn't know the actual number. Hearst passed away in 1891, and Head dropped out, but Haggin and Tevis continued to own and operate the Victorio Land and Cattle Company as one piece of their gigantic Kern County Land Company.

A combination of historical and ecological factors enabled the Gray to retain its natural integrity over the past century. It remained in Kern Company ownership until 1970, when it was bought by another large land and cattle operation. This meant that throughout its history, when drought struck the Gray Ranch, its owners could easily move the cattle off to greener pastures somewhere else (or to the Kern Company's feedlots near Bakersfield). In the dry years of the 1930s, the herd on the Gray shrank by two-thirds, from 18,000 to 6,000 head. In the next severe drought, in the 1950s, it contracted still further, to a mere 1,300 mother cows. Cuts such as these were made out of necessity as much as prudence. The Gray had relatively few water sources, and most of them were earthen tanks that filled only from surface run-off. In a drought, the tanks usually dried up long before the grass ran out. The worst excesses of overgrazing during drought were for these reasons avoided.

Even when overgrazing did occur, the Gray was protected from shrub encroachment by other factors. Mesquite trees cannot survive temperatures below 12 degrees Fahrenheit, and the Animas valley, with an elevation around 5,000 feet, routinely crosses this threshold in the winter. Fire also played a significant role, especially at higher elevations. Water sources were most limited in the mountains, meaning that cattle were scarce, grasses abundant, and lightning fires common. These fires were generally not suppressed, because in 1952 the Kern Company completed a land swap with the Forest Service that converted the Animas division of the Coronado National Forest into private land. Had the Animas Mountains remained in Forest Service ownership, fire suppression would have been much more aggressive in the name of protecting the ponderosa pine, southwestern white pine, and Douglas fir timber that shrouds its crest. Instead, fires produced a mosaic of burned and unburned patches all the way up to Animas Peak. In the region, only a few ranges in Mexico have retained a fire regime closer to the evolutionary norm.

In 1967 the Kern County Land Company was acquired by Tenneco Corporation, a pipeline and petroleum conglomerate based in Houston. Tenneco West, as the new firm was called, quickly began selling off Diamond A lands. The Pacific Western Land Company, a subsidiary of Phelps-Dodge Copper Company, bought the eastern side of the Gray Ranch in connection with its smelter in the Playas Valley. Then the Phoenix-based partnership of Wayne Pruett and Peter Wray bought the rest of the Gray in December of 1970 for $6 million, simultaneously acquiring the Diamond A brand and rights to the Victorio name. They reorganized their venture capital firm as the Victorio Company, and over the ensuing decade they bought up other ranch lands surrounding the Gray and secured long-term leases to graze on Pacific Western's holdings.

The new Victorio Company combined livestock production with rural real estate speculation and tax shelters for outside capital. At a time when the highest bracket paid income taxes of 50 percent, ranches were an accountant's dream. The vast majority of the purchase price (sometimes nearly 100 percent) could be attributed by appraisal to capital improvements—

fences, wells, stock tanks, pipelines, ranch houses, and so forth—and thus amortized on seven-year depreciation schedules, even though most of these structures had much longer useful life spans. A ranch that broke even, or made a small return, served on paper as a large, ongoing income tax write-off. Victorio's records for the Gray Ranch, for example, show losses every year but one from 1970 to 1980, resulting in tax reductions as large as half a million dollars. After depreciating the original investment, one could either make further improvements or sell out, usually at a handsome profit. If one flipped the proceeds into another ranch, even the capital gains could be deferred. The whole system might have inflated into a speculative bubble and popped, except that population growth in much of the West was so high that underlying property values had a real basis for appreciation as well.

FOR SALE

Victorio owned half a dozen other large ranches across the West, along with many smaller ones and a number of commercial properties in Denver and Los Angeles. It was these latter investments that brought the company down in the stagflation of the late 1970s and early 1980s.

Gathering horses on the Gray Ranch prior to fall roundup.

Caught in a cash-flow trap, in 1981 Victorio took a $25 million loan from the American Breco Company, a Los Angeles firm owned by Mexican billionaire Pablo Brenner. Victorio settled this debt two years later by forfeiting the Gray and another large ranch, the Buenos Aires, an hour south of Tucson. Looking to recover his losses, Brenner stocked the ranches heavily with steers, which could be liquidated rapidly, and put the Gray and the Buenos Aires up for sale. The U.S. Fish and Wildlife Service quickly expressed interest in both.

The Buenos Aires was another major desert grassland ranch, but it was by far the lesser of the two properties. It was barely one-third the size and harbored far less biological diversity than the Gray. In the 1880s it too had been dominated by native perennial grasses, but grazing and drought had converted it into a mesquite scrubland by the 1950s. In the 1970s, Victorio spent millions of dollars to bulldoze the mesquites and seed grasses, resulting in another transformation, this time to a near-monotype of Lehmann lovegrass, an African

The late Tom Day, a long-time cowboy in the Borderlands.

species imported by the U.S. Department of Agriculture for use in rangeland revegetation. In addition, 80 percent of the Buenos Aires was leased from the Arizona State Land Department.

Two factors made the Buenos Aires a higher priority for the Fish and Wildlife Service nonetheless. It was where ongoing work had shown promise for restoring the masked bobwhite quail, one of the nation's original listed endangered species and the object of intense political interest. The bulldozing and other work Victorio did briefly made the Buenos Aires into suitable habitat for captive-bred masked bobwhites, and it looked as though a bird once considered extinct might miraculously be restored. Ornithologists declared the masked bobwhite "Arizona's most famous bird," and environmental groups mobilized to promote the idea of turning the ranch into a refuge. The Buenos Aires was also much closer than the Gray to a large metropolitan area, making it both more vulnerable to real estate development and more accessible to visitors. In 1985, the Fish and Wildlife Service purchased the ranch and transformed it into the Buenos Aires National Wildlife Refuge, with a major emphasis on "public use"—that is, recreation and tourism. Concurrently, plans were drawn up for the Gray to become the Animas National Wildlife Refuge.

According to some sources, Pablo Brenner was so annoyed with the Fish and Wildlife Service after selling the Buenos Aires that he refused to negotiate with them on the Gray. There were other potential bidders, including a Sri Lankan investor who reportedly offered $22.5 million and wished to convert large areas of the ranch to fruit orchards. The Nature Conservancy offered to purchase an option on the Gray early in 1989, hoping to secure the ranch against other bidders and then raise money to buy it. But Brenner did not reply, apparently wanting to sell the ranch outright instead of an option. Then, in December, he gave the Conservancy two weeks to sign a contract at a non-negotiable price of $18 million.

In a hastily organized conference call of the national board of directors, the decision was made to do it. The rationale was simple and somewhat desperate: This is why we exist—if we don't do it, we forsake our principles.

When the deal closed in January 1990, it catapulted the Gray Ranch onto the national stage. The *New York Times* reported that it was the largest acquisition in the Conservancy's forty-year history and quoted a Conservancy official as saying that the Gray harbored more kinds of mammals than "any existing national wildlife refuge or national park in the continental United States." That summer, the *Times* ran a feature story in its Sunday magazine, elaborating on the Gray's biological diversity and describing it as the largest conservation transaction in U.S. history. "Now the question," wrote reporter Bruce Selcraig, "seems to be *how many* people will get to see it?" The Conservancy had ordered a 50 percent stock reduction but retained the cowboys and foreman Lonnie Moore to continue the cattle operation. Beyond that, Selcraig reported, plans were still under review. John Sawhill pronounced the Gray among the world's most beautiful places, and soon it was a centerpiece of the "last great places" campaign for biodiversity conservation.

Local reactions to the transaction were far from jubilant, however. "You might as well have told us the Martians had landed," was Bill McDonald's description some years later. The only virtue of the Conservancy, in the neighbors' eyes, was that it wasn't the federal government. In newspapers and cafes, the deal was decried as further evidence that outside interests were taking over the countryside and displacing ranchers. One local remarked to Selcraig acerbically: "There'll be people from the East and people from universities who have read some books coming down here telling us how to conserve things." Perceptions were based partly on face-to-face encounters and thus varied with the individuals involved. Bill McDonald recalls an early Conservancy presentation about the Gray that struck him as condescending in its tone regarding ranchers and ranching. Lonnie Moore, who had managed the Gray since 1983, told the *Times*: "I think I can trust that Bonnivier guy. He's from Idaho and knows cattle. But I don't have much use for Bell." (Guy Bonnivier was the Conservancy's Gray Ranch project director at the time. Gary Bell was a Conservancy ecologist.)

FOR SALE, AGAIN

The Conservancy didn't expect to own the Gray for long. Selling to the Fish and Wildlife Service was Plan A, and national environmental groups pressured the Conservancy strenuously to convey the Gray into public ownership. Nothing short of that, they argued, could do justice to this crown jewel of biological diversity. For all its diversity, however, the Gray did not have a celebrated endangered species like the masked bobwhite, and no ardent in-state constituency emerged in support of converting it into a refuge. Instead, New Mexicans of all stripes rallied against the idea. Local and national cattlegrowers' associations accused the Conservancy of being little more than an acquisitions agent for the federal government. The prospect of taking such a large piece of private land off the tax rolls aroused strong protests, especially in Hidalgo County. The Fish and Wildlife Service pledged to make payments far in excess of the ranch's property taxes and insisted that refuge expenditures would bolster the local economy, but few were persuaded. The copper smelter at nearby Playas was the county's largest employer, and many people objected that a refuge might foreclose future development of important mineral resources. Most basically, though, locals felt that a refuge would threaten the day-to-day feel of the area. When it was learned that the Service anticipated thirty to sixty thousand visitors per year, the community reacted vehemently. Bill McDonald, in his capacity as head of the local cattlegrowers' association, helped organize letters and phone calls to elected officials to protest the idea. It happened that Secretary of the Interior Manuel Lujan was a native New Mexican, and without his signature the sale could not occur. He indicated he would not consent, and the Conservancy's New Mexico chapter board eventually decided that selling the Gray to the federal government was not an option they could pursue. Joe Williams, chair of the national board at the time, concurred. Some other solution was needed.

In the meantime, what do you do with one of the world's last great places? You study it, of course. The ranch was soon crawling with scientists eager to document its treasures. As private land, it had never been generally accessible to researchers, and for many, just the chance to set foot on the Gray was enticement enough. Proposals poured in from professors and graduate students across the country: bees, birds, bats, cacti, snakes, grasses, rodents, soils, geology, archaeology, herbivores, predators—you name it, someone wanted to study it. In addition, the Conservancy secured a multi-year grant from the MacArthur Foundation to research the biological diversity of the Gray and develop a plan for conservation in the Borderlands region. Contracts were signed to investigate fire history and forest structure in the Animas and other mountain ranges. Wetland sediments were explored for evidence of past vegetation conditions. Inventories were completed and entered into databases. Rare lowland leopard frogs were documented on the Gray, as well as the only known extant populations of the Chiricahua mudwort. Endangered nectar-feeding bats were found to be more abundant than expected. Statistical models were developed to predict the distribution of biological diversity across gradients of elevation, geology, and climate. In just a few years, the scientific knowledge base regarding the Gray Ranch and the Borderlands ballooned.

But the Conservancy had more troublesome questions to answer: how to run the place, and most importantly, how to pay for it? It had borrowed the funds to buy the ranch from its own reserves, and repayment had to be made with interest. The interest alone was nearly $2 million per year—roughly double what the Victorio Company had typically grossed from a herd of cattle far larger than the Conservancy wished to run. Fundraising was difficult, as well—donors prefer to give gifts that make a purchase possible, not that repay an internal loan after the fact. Without the federal government as a potential buyer, the Conservancy soon realized that the Gray was becoming a fiscal sinkhole. In the spring of 1991, Sawhill took the ranch "off line," removing it from the normal chain of management authority that ran through the New Mexico chapter. Instead, the future of the Gray would be determined directly from the Conservancy's headquarters in Arlington, Virginia. Sawhill delegated the job to John Cook, a vice president working in the national office.

JOHN COOK

Cook headed west without a trace of ranching background, an unlikely choice to figure out the future of this enormous, politically charged property. Lanky, pale, and bespectacled, he looked every bit like the born-and-bred New Englander that he is. (He lives and breathes for the Boston Red Sox and the New England Patriots.) Renowned in Conservancy circles for his fundraising prowess, Cook clothes the utmost seriousness and efficiency in habits of boyish bemusement. He had no illusions about retaining the Gray, and no particular idea what would happen.

Cook tapped Mike Dennis and Ben Brown to assist him. An attorney with a striking Boston accent, Dennis worked in the Arlington office as a real estate and conservation easement specialist. Brown was a conservation biologist with expertise in rangelands, particularly the grasslands of the Great Plains. He had spent the preceding years helping the Conservancy evaluate Western ranch properties for possible acquisition. Law, real estate,

John Cook.

and science—these were the basic pieces Cook had to work with. According to Dennis, Sawhill gave them unusual authority to resolve the Gray "unencumbered by bureaucracy." The debt was mounting, and "someone had to take responsibility for this project." The team took stock of the research program, clamped down on access, and began to evaluate the livestock operation. Then they set their sights on finding an appropriate buyer, someone who would honor the Gray's unsurpassed conservation values while freeing the Conservancy of the burden of managing it and paying it off.

The Gray's size was an asset from an ecological perspective, since it brought a wide range of habitats into a single, unfragmented unit. But it was a liability if one were trying to sell the ranch. It made the property prohibitively expensive for most potential buyers, who tended to see some parts of the ranch as more valuable than others. For anyone who wanted to raise livestock, for example, the

Animas Mountains were not worth buying: With so much grass in the foothills and valley bottoms, why tie up millions of dollars to own acres that your animals might never even graze? Even a developer couldn't make the Gray pencil out as a single, up-front purchase, since it would take too long to sell so much private land in small pieces. No one seemed interested in the whole thing.

Recognizing this, Cook drafted a status report in May 1991 that proposed to divide the ranch into three management areas, with different potential ownership and management futures for each. A "core natural area" would encompass the Animas Mountains, ensuring "uncompromised protection" for "the best occurrences of the globally important ecological values of the ranch." This part of the Gray—about 45,000 acres in all—would not be grazed and would either remain in Conservancy ownership or be sold to a public agency. A slightly larger "conservation management area" would buffer the core,

Gray Ranch cowboys saddling for afternoon work.

and might be sold to either a public or a private entity. Grazing would occur there if it were compatible with conservation goals. Finally, nearly half the ranch, mostly lower-elevation grasslands, would be designated "range" and marketed to private buyers for livestock grazing under "best practice range management." Research and recreation would occur on the core and conservation areas but not on the range. According to the report, the Conservancy was open to any combination of ownership and management scenarios within this framework.

The 1991 status report proposed a geographical solution to what John Cook describes as "the unenviable position of being exquisitely caught between two rocks with only a hard place as a landing net." Lines would be drawn on a map and fences built on the ground. Half the ranch would remain in livestock production, satisfying the cattlegrowers' associations and the private property advocates; half would be "protected," satisfying the environmental groups and federal land management agencies such as the Fish and Wildlife Service. The two philosophies would meet, if at all, in the conservation management area, which combined elements of both.

The status report framed this proposal in larger terms, however, insisting that "protection" versus "economic use" was a false dichotomy. "The Conservancy believes that the challenge to conserve and protect biological diversity effectively lies in society's ability to accommodate both the protection of our ecological resources *and* compatible economic activity. This is the only way whole and functioning ecosystems can survive one hundred or more years from now." The "Last Great Places" initiative was based on this premise, and the Gray Ranch was the first major acquisition of the program; as such, "its use, management, and ownership will be the first and crucial test of our ability to forge significant new partnerships useful not only in southern New Mexico but throughout the United States and beyond." The Conservancy was actively recruiting both public and private partners "to make the vision of

compatible economic use and natural areas protection a reality," beginning with the Gray. Given the political climate, a private partner needed to be found first.

For several months in late 1991 it looked like Ted Turner would become that partner. Through his foundation, he was actively involved in endangered species conservation, and he already owned several large ranches in New Mexico. He had converted some of them from cattle to bison operations in an effort to restore more natural patterns of grazing and kick-start an alternative to the beef industry. There was little evidence that bison had ever grazed in the Animas Valley, however (although more evidence has since been found). Negotiations proceeded through the fall, and John and his team began work on a conservation easement to accompany the sale. But Turner decided not to proceed.

Early in 1992, when word spread that Turner was not going to buy the Gray, Drum Hadley invited John Cook to Guadalupe Canyon. John had heard of Drum and knew of his family background, but he had not met him and had been told that he probably never would. For that matter, he hadn't met any of the ranchers in the area. He had had his hands full on the Gray, and they had followed a time-honored, unwritten rule of ranch country: you stay out of my business and I'll stay out of yours.

The drive from Gray Ranch headquarters to Guadalupe Canyon is a long one, tracing three-quarters of a complete circle around the southern half of the Peloncillo Mountains to the mouth of Guadalupe Canyon. From there, John bumped up a five-mile dirt road to Drum's house, crisscrossing the creek under tall cottonwoods, sycamores, hackberries, and willows. Drum had brought Guadalupe Creek back to life over his twenty years there. The results had earned him the New Mexico Nature Conservancy's Aldo Leopold Award the year before; now, they earned him instant credibility in the eyes of Cook.

On horseback one can travel a shorter route, and it was that area that Drum had on his mind when he and

John first met. Every spring the Hadleys drove their cattle up Guadalupe Canyon to their easternmost pasture, overlooking the Animas Valley, and each year the view that greeted them upon cresting the divide took their breath away. The far south end of the Gray is a vast Pleistocene lakebed that straddles the border with Mexico. Dead flat and nothing but grass, the lake pasture seems to pool the sunlight and glow, much as it once, in a wetter climate, pooled water from the surrounding mountains. Drum liked to strike awe into friends, reporters, and even his own children by instructing them to close their eyes for a few seconds as their horses surmounted the ridge to behold the view. A neighboring ranch had nearly been subdivided recently, and Drum was concerned that this area and this view might soon be lost. His neighbors had entreated him to buy the Gray, but he was more interested in adding the lake pasture to his own ranch. He asked John about buying just the southern end.

In the months he'd been working there, John had begun to reconsider the wisdom of dividing the Gray at all. There was talk of introducing California condors into the Animas Mountains, and John knew this would require special management of hunting in the surrounding grasslands to ensure no lead bullets ended up in a condor's belly. The Conservancy wanted to ensure that fire would have a role on the Gray into the future, and this too would be easier if it remained in a single ownership. These were just two examples, but they raised the broader question whether its great size was part of what had kept the Gray so ecologically intact through the past century. Of course, keeping it in one piece put John back between two rocks and a hard place: how to answer the competing demands of the environmentalist-agency proponents and the private land-ranching groups, and how to find someone who could afford the whole ranch.

As it turned out, offering to divide the Gray was a Solomonic solution, and it was Drum's son, Seth, who proposed a way to keep it whole. The extended Hadley family would establish a nonprofit operating foundation to buy the Gray, encumbered by a conservation easement protecting its ecological values and forbidding subdivision. The Conservancy would hold the easement, whose value would be deducted from the purchase price. It took two years to close the deal. Just selling a ranch as large as the Gray was a complicated matter; the Conservancy and the Hadleys also had to craft the conservation easement and put together the foundation. For months the negotiations remained a secret, even from neighboring ranchers.

CONSERVATION RANCHING

In lieu of a geographical compromise, the Hadleys' proposal involved mating conservation to human use on the same piece of land: Ranching had to be conservation, and vice versa. On top of that, the arrangement had to be translated into legally binding contracts. How should the conservation values of the ranch be defined and protected under the easement? Should the focus be on the grazing operation—setting stocking rates, prohibiting overgrazing, and so on—or on broader indicators of ecological condition such as plant cover and diversity? What about enforcement and procedures for resolving disputes? How could human-caused impacts such as overgrazing be reliably distinguished from natural disturbances such as drought? John and Drum wrestled with all these questions, assisted by Mike, Ben, Seth, and a small squadron of lawyers, scientists, and advisers.

So much depended on the confidence each side placed in the other. Would the foundation try to run more cattle than the Conservancy felt comfortable with? Would the Conservancy enforce the easement capriciously, or in such a way that grazing became effectively

Although lush and green from summer rains, this site had burned not long before the photograph was taken.

impossible? If either side felt the need, they could dream up more "worst case scenarios" than could ever be pre-empted by legal language inserted into the easement. Only a growing sense of shared commitment kept the Hadleys and the Conservancy at the table. Eventually the group took as its mantra a statement Drum made one day when they were discussing each party's rights in the event that the easement were violated: "We are going to do what's right for the *land*!" Gradually, each side became more confident that the other was working in good faith and that both were converging on a shared vision of conservation ranching backed up by rigorous science.

As John Cook's confidence in the Hadleys grew, it became harder to insist on continued Conservancy presence in the management of the Gray. For a partnership to work, it had to be a partnership of equals. Selling anything less than the whole ranch, or selling it with lots of strings attached, would send a message of less-than-complete confidence; it would be disrespectful, at least in the eyes of the community. In the end, no strictures were placed on livestock grazing in the easement: those decisions lie entirely in the hands of the Animas Foundation. The Conservancy chose instead to monitor ecological conditions, primarily based on vegetation, once every five years. The results are compared to a baseline completed at the time of sale, and the easement simply requires Animas to maintain or improve on the baseline conditions, taking into account variables beyond their control such as drought. Public access raised analogous issues. There was strong sentiment, especially outside the Conservancy, that the general public should obtain some claim to the ranch, if not for recreation than at least for science. In its negotiations with Turner, the Conservancy had proposed retaining a parcel of land for a field station and access rights to conduct research, especially in the Animas Mountains. Under the new deal, the Animas Foundation would have research, education, and outreach built into its mission, and the Conservancy would have access rights only to monitor the easement. All day-to-day management authority, including public access, was transferred to Animas.

Early in 1993, the parties publicly announced their agreement. The newly formed Animas Foundation would pay $13.2 million, reflecting a $4.8 million value for the easement. Its mission statement was to "encourage the practice of a land ethic to preserve, heal, restore, and sustain wildlands and waters, their inhabitants and cultures." The deal closed in mid-1994.

It was a significant new direction for The Nature Conservancy, and the transaction once again put the Gray Ranch in the headlines. Previously, the Conservancy had focused on creating preserves: areas where human activities were restricted to research and limited tourism. But Sawhill had proposed a new philosophy after assuming his post in 1989. If the lands outside of protected areas were not managed well, he argued, preserves would eventually be inadequate to protect biological diversity. "It's not good enough anymore to fence nature away from people," he told Alan Weisman of the *Los Angeles Times*. Elsewhere he wrote: "The time when we could think of protecting the environment and excluding people has long since ended; the 'museum' model of conservation simply does not take into account the very real needs of human beings. What will work for the future—what we must do—is to include people in planning for conservation, so that environmental protection is not viewed as having come at their expense." The Gray Ranch was the Conservancy's first major act in the name of this new philosophy.

Unlike in 1990, however, local people viewed the transaction favorably. Some ranchers in the area would continue to view the Conservancy with suspicion for years to come, but most saw the sale of the Gray to the Animas Foundation as a huge step in the right direction. Bill McDonald wrote a column for the Douglas *Daily Dispatch* in which he described the deal as "a mighty blow" that augured well for ranching and conservation alike. "The Animas Foundation is saying that this huge area of private land will remain rural. But it will not become sterile for any species: plant, animal or human." In choosing to sell to a private entity rather than the government, McDonald wrote, the Conservancy had turned away from an approach to conservation that "usually has one result that mirrors development: the displacement of those people who live on and sustain themselves from the land." For the core group of Malpai ranchers, John Cook had endorsed by example Jim Corbett's position that a "viable land ethic" had to be based on genuine, voluntary partnership among equals. He had put Sawhill's words into action.

To write his column, Bill McDonald phoned John Cook in Arlington for an interview. "You don't know me, but I know all about you," he said. John had earned Drum's confidence, and Drum in turn encouraged his neighbors to open their doors to John. Bill invited him to visit the Sycamore Ranch and go for a ride. Once again, John drove over the Peloncillos and dropped into the San Bernardino Valley, turned, and bumped up a long driveway to a low adobe house tucked on a bench of land above a dry creek bed. They rode through one big open landscape, as far as John could see, but Bill pointed out the complexities: this is private land, now we're on BLM property, that's state land, through this gate it's national forest. The difficulties of managing such a mosaic of

landownership types, and the ecological absurdity of not managing them together, became increasingly clear to John. All of the challenges he had foreseen for a divided Gray Ranch were ever-present realities for Bill and his neighbors, not to mention the agencies. Then Bill asked him a question: "We want to put fire back into this land—can The Nature Conservancy help?" When all the area landowners gathered at the Malpai Ranch to discuss fire in March 1993, John attended as well, partially incognito: Drum and the Glenns introduced him to their neighbors not as a Conservancy official but simply as a friend.

———

One of the first official acts of the Animas Foundation was to host the meeting of Malpai ranchers and government agencies in April 1993, described in the previous chapter. The circumstances surrounding the Gray cannot but have helped get the attention of the invited agency representatives (and their supervisors). Likewise, the unity of the ranching community and the clarity of its message, attained through the meetings of the preceding two years, can only have helped to persuade the agencies that the request for collaborative management was a genuine invitation. In short, the Gray Ranch leveraged a degree of recognition and credibility for the Malpai Agenda that might otherwise have taken years to achieve. The unexpected, improbable sale of the ranch to the Animas Foundation made it possible to reevaluate old prejudices and presuppositions: If the Conservancy was no longer untrustworthy in the eyes of the Malpai ranchers, the Malpai ranchers were now more trustworthy in the eyes of the agencies.

By entrusting the Animas Foundation with the entirety of the Gray Ranch and corresponding management authority, John Cook earned the Conservancy an invitation to remain in the Borderlands as a partner in

Malpai's efforts to restore fire and prevent subdivision. Some of the neighboring ranchers were uncomfortable about working with the Conservancy and withdrew, but the McDonalds, the Glenns, and the Hadleys believed in John both as a friend and as someone with significant skills to contribute. John accepted their invitation and asked Sawhill to extend his assignment in the area. Beginning in the spring of 1993 they met frequently to discuss how to proceed. Initially they envisioned the Animas Foundation taking up the Malpai Agenda, but they soon realized that an independent entity was needed, one whose focus was the larger landscape rather than just the Gray Ranch.

The ranchers were experienced at working together, but they were not familiar with the intricate details of nonprofit organizations, fundraising, and foundations, or tax and easement law. These were arenas in which John and Mike Dennis were exceptionally skilled, and in less than a year the Malpai Borderlands Group was incorporated as a tax-exempt, nonprofit organization that could accept donations, apply for grants, and hold conservation easements. The Nature Conservancy and the Animas Foundation each donated $1 million to seed the effort—money that the Group has held in reserve in case they someday need to purchase a ranch to prevent it from subdividing. Bill felt they had to find an executive director whom the state and federal agencies would take seriously; Drum and John agreed and suggested that Bill himself was the person for the job. Bill then asked John to co-direct the Malpai Group with him. He recalls looking furtively around as he walked into the Conservancy's national headquarters in Arlington for the first time, unavoidably conspicuous in his cowboy boots and hat. He wasn't certain which was less believable: that he was there or that they were letting him in.

PAGES 68–69: *Prehistoric pictographs in the northern Peloncillo Mountains.*

Until very recently we have administered the southern Arizona Forests on the assumption that while overgrazing was bad for erosion, fire was worse, and that therefore we must keep the brush hazard grazed down to the extent necessary to prevent serious fires. In making this assumption we have accepted the traditional theory as to the place of fire and forests in erosion, and rejected the plain story written on the face of Nature.

—ALDO LEOPOLD,
JOURNAL OF FORESTRY, 1924

CHAPTER 3

GRAZING, FIRE, AND DROUGHT IN THE BORDERLANDS

There is very little to be said about this range except that it is in excellent condition[,] is under good management and [is] well cared for by the permittees. We have a fire hazard there now.
—FOREST RANGER D. S. MARKS, MEMO
TO COTTONWOOD ALLOTMENT FILE, APRIL 1932

Across the bottom of D. S. Marks's 1932 memo is a handwritten line, presumably added by a supervisor.

"We'll take a chance on the fires," it says. His initials are partially illegible—C. M., I think—but the purpose of the memo is easy to see. Marks was alerting his superiors to the risk of fire in the Cottonwood Basin, the upper portion of the McDonald family's Sycamore Ranch in the Peloncillo Mountains. By adding his note, C. M. acknowledged that the alert had been received and thereby relieved Marks of any responsibility should a fire occur. Perhaps C. M. had read Aldo Leopold's famous paper from eight years before, "Grass, Brush, Timber, and Fire in Southern

to change in his own time, and C. M.'s note may be a small indication that it had. If so, however, that trend was soon reversed, or at least stopped. The contradiction between Forest Service grazing and fire-management policies in the Southwest persisted for at least fifty years after Leopold wrote, and even today it has been resolved only at a few isolated locations. Catalyzed by a suppressed fire, the Malpai Borderlands Group represents a grassroots call to resolve the contradiction by abandoning the goal of outright fire prevention. Fires cannot be prevented in this landscape, they argue, except perhaps at the cost of complete degradation of grasslands and watersheds. The only question is what kind of fires to have: how often, how intense, and at what risk to people, property, and the environment.

The next three chapters examine Malpai's efforts to conserve grasslands and restore fire, protect endangered species and biological diversity, and prevent subdivision and development of private lands in the area. Each is an interrelated part of the

Arizona," and had taken its conclusions to heart. Taking chances was not the Forest Service's normal stance regarding fire, and C. M. was indeed taking a personal and professional risk. He was also implicitly recognizing a contradiction in national forest policies as applied to Southwestern rangelands: Achieving one goal of those policies—good grazing management—tended to undermine another—preventing fires.

Leopold's use of the words "until very recently" implies that the Forest Service's position had begun whole: to conserve grasslands and diversity requires restoring fire; to restore fire requires preventing subdivision; to prevent subdivision requires maintaining the economic viability of ranching, which in turn requires conserving grasslands and diversity. They are strands that the Malpai Group is attempting to braid together into a single rope, which may unravel and fail if any one of them is removed. The strength of the rope and the challenge of reconstituting it cannot be assessed, however, without first understanding the longer history of grazing, fire, and drought in the Borderlands. How and why did fire disappear, and what effects did its disappearance have? What have scientists learned about fire, and how has scientific knowledge affected actual land management? Ultimately these questions are not only ecological but also political ones, central to the "viable land ethic" espoused in the Malpai Agenda. As fire historian and former Forest Service firefighter Stephen Pyne writes, "Good citizens use fire well; bad ones, poorly or not at all."

THE CATTLE BOOM

The Malpai Borderlands were the last redoubt of Apache resistance to the U.S. military. Most Apaches were moved onto the San Carlos Reservation beginning in 1876, but for another ten years bands of warriors refused to be settled in this way. Instead, they took refuge in the rugged mountain ranges from the Mogollon Rim south into the Sierra Madre, moving back and forth across the Mexican border in a prolonged game of cat-and-mouse with the two nations' armies. Only when U.S. forces pursued them deep into the Sierra Madre did they agree to give up the fight, and in 1886 Geronimo came back to Skeleton Canyon in the Peloncillo Mountains and surrendered. It was the end of a very long war. Skirmishes with Spanish and Mexican troops had been ongoing for the better part of two hundred years. Generations of Apaches had ambushed caravans and raided settlements for horses, cattle, arms, and provisions, perpetuating a regional atmosphere of instability, violence, and reprisal.

As a result of the Apache wars, the Borderlands remained largely uninhabited until late in the nineteenth century. There had been short periods of relative peace, when missionaries, army commanders, and settlers had extended their activities eastward from Tucson into what is now called, appropriately enough, Cochise County. Like Ignacio Ortiz's San Bernardino Ranch, however, these outposts had been abandoned when the raiding and violence resumed. When peaceful conditions were finally secured in the 1880s, Anglo-American ranchers moved in from places such as Texas, Pennsylvania, California, New England, or even old England, seizing what appeared to be untouched, unclaimed land. Whatever the Spanish or the Mexicans might have taught them about grazing livestock in this landscape was effectively lost or ignored.

What the new ranchers beheld upon their arrival was open grassland valleys, interrupted by trees only along creeks and washes or by patches of brush or cacti on particularly rocky or nutrient-poor soils. The overall aspect resembled the short-grass prairies of Texas or Colorado—prime cattle country. If the grasses were rich, however, most of the ranchers were not. They borrowed money to buy their livestock, often at rates upwards of 12 percent, and hoped that their herds reproduced and grew more quickly than the interest. If things went well—the rains fell, the cows had calves, the calves grew fat, and prices stayed high—this was easily done, and for roughly twenty years things went remarkably well: The number of cattle in Arizona increased from fewer than 50,000 in 1870 to about 1.5 million in 1891. In the midst of the boom, the Territorial governor waxed rhapsodic:

In Arizona a day without bright sunshine is so rare as to be remarkable, and every month in the year cattle run on their ranges and find no lack of feed. These favorable climatic conditions make Arizona the stock-raisers' paradise… With its magnificent climate and abundance of pasture, its large natural increase and small percentage of loss, this Territory can produce beef more cheaply than any grazing region in the United States…

The governor's judgments were not so much inaccurate as incomplete. Many of the grass species had indeed evolved with bison in the Great Plains and had become adapted to periodic grazing. But the mild winters in the Southwest—which seemed an advantage for ranchers after the deadly Great Plains blizzards of the 1880s—had a potential downside as well. Plants could grow at any time of year, provided it rained, but the prime forage species—perennial bunchgrasses such as blue grama, black grama, bush muhly, and plains lovegrass—grew only in the summer. Many shrubs, in contrast, grew year-round. The shrubs were also more drought-tolerant than the grasses by virtue of deeper roots, and early ranchers had no idea how frequent and ferocious Southwestern droughts could be.

What the governor and ranchers failed to recognize was that periodic fires were necessary to give the grasses an edge over the shrubs. Both kinds of plants had adapted to withstand prolonged drought and then capitalize on brief wet conditions to reproduce and store up moisture or nutrients for the next dry spell.

A view of the Chiricahua Mountains from the upper San Bernardino Valley.

The result was bursts of biomass that eventually had to go somewhere, by consumption or decomposition. May and June cooked it like a kiln drier, and the monsoon, even when it failed to bring much moisture, almost always brought lightning. Fire did little harm to grass plants because their growth points are at ground level, below the most intense heat, but it killed seedling shrubs, which grow from their tips. Studies of tree rings from throughout the Southwest reveal a strong pattern going back more than one thousand years: Fire was most abundant when severe drought followed a year or more of above normal rains. Any given site burned once every five to fifteen years. Without these fires, the Southwest's desert grasslands would not have been grasslands at all.

When the rains failed between 1891 and the summer of 1893, the whole system came tumbling down. Selling out at depressed prices was tantamount to defaulting, and many ranchers opted to hold onto their livestock and pray. An estimated 50 to 75 percent of cattle died of hunger or thirst. The range was reduced to dirt, except in places so far from water that the cattle couldn't get there. Even where grasses remained, their ability to recover from grazing was crippled. They needed more time and more moisture than usual, but they could not get the time because the ranchers had no control over where their livestock went. In the absence of fences, any rancher who cut his herd watched someone else's show up to graze. At the first moisture, everyone restocked, even if more debt had to be assumed to do so.

A vicious cycle ensued. Without good grass cover, the soil could not hold rain as effectively, evaporation and run-off rates increased, and the plants got less moisture when they needed more. Erosion carried away the most nutrient-rich soils, in an area where topsoil is measured in millimeters, not inches. When the droughts were broken by torrential rain falling on bare ground, the flooding was unlike anything anyone had known before.

Creeks and rivers ran so high, weighted with so much sediment, that floodplains gave way altogether. Steep-sided channels known as arroyos formed to accommodate the flow. Farm fields, roads, buildings, and bridges were carried away. Once formed, the arroyos became permanent features of the landscape, lowering alluvial water tables and further accelerating the transport of rainwater away from wherever it fell. These interlocking feedbacks exacerbated the underlying contradiction of the Cattle Boom: grasses grew irregularly over time, whereas the ranchers' debts came due every year.

Meanwhile, the disrupted fire regime began to tip the competitive balance in favor of shrubs. Even if lightning happened to strike where some grass was present, the resulting fire could not travel far without running into bare ground. Although a few ranchers recognized the value of fire, most did not mourn the loss, viewing fire as a competitor with their animals for the grass. Some commentators associated fire with the "savage" Apaches—who had burned for hunting, warfare, and other purposes—and considered its disappearance evidence of advancing civilization. Even the fact that fires had once been common appears to have been quickly forgotten, especially among newcomers and urban residents.

Three broad sets of changes followed the devastation of the turn of the twentieth century. The soils and plants were rearranged, in some ways immediately and in others over the course of decades. New laws were passed that ended the open public domain and transferred ownership and administration of large parts of the range to new state and federal agencies. And a new science was summoned into being, largely at the behest of the federal government and drawing on the fledgling field of plant ecology. The scientists worked to understand the changes in the soils and the plants, and the agencies worked to translate the scientists' findings into policies and procedures for ranchers, who would henceforth lease much of their range. By a combination of political forces, economic constraints, and scientific misapplications, the resulting system would solve certain problems only by making others worse.

RANGE SCIENCE

In the aftermath of the Cattle Boom, the Southwest was judged to be the most severely impacted region of the country, and the very first federally funded range research was conducted there. Early studies estimated that carrying capacities—the number of livestock the range could support—declined by more than 40 percent in Texas, and even more in Arizona and New Mexico.

Research done on the Santa Rita Experimental Range, south of Tucson, Arizona, and the Jornada Experimental Range, outside Las Cruces, New Mexico—founded in 1903 and 1912, respectively—helped set the course of twentieth-century range science. The goal was to restore the range to its "original capacity"—an obvious and understandable ambition that still has strong adherents today. But it already contained some faulty assumptions.

The first assumption was embedded in the term itself: namely, that some determinate carrying capacity existed at all in a region of such highly variable rainfall. Countless studies were done to determine the number of

Herpetologists Cecil Schwalbe (left, holding a horned lizard) and Phil Rosen (right) have worked closely with rancher Matt Magoffin (center) and the Malpai Group to study and protect the Chiricahua leopard frog.

Variegated fritillary butterfly.

cattle that should be permitted on rangelands of various kinds and qualities. Old-time ranchers were asked how many head their ranges had supported before the boom collapsed, and their answers helped set benchmarks of "original" capacity. Then, measurements were taken at research sites such as the Santa Rita and Jornada Experimental Ranges, and calculations were performed: so many pounds of forage per acre per year, minus the amount that should be left so the plants can recover, divided by the intake requirements of an average cow. The result was called "actual" capacity. The first such figure for southeastern Arizona was published in 1910: 37 acres per head, or about 17 head per square mile. The idea was that by stocking at actual capacity, one would avoid overgrazing and thus permit gradual recovery toward original capacity.

The focus on carrying capacities reflected the fact that the major political decision had already been made, as contained in the Public Lands Commission's 1905 report. Grazing lands on the national forests would be divided into allotments and leased to individual ranchers for their exclusive use. The political goal was maximum bona fide settlement, so the challenge was to allocate the range in pieces large enough to support a ranching household, and no larger. This meant large enough to support a herd of a certain minimum size. The number had to be static, because each allotment would have to be fenced to ensure exclusive use by the permittee, and the fences could not be moved once built.

There were economic constraints at work as well. Livestock ranching was heavily dependent on credit—even more so than crop agriculture—and this was recognized as a major source of instability in the industry. Indebted ranchers were prone to stock heavily and to resist destocking during drought, because their cattle were their only significant capital asset. Some means of capitalizing the land, short of outright privatization, was needed to give ranchers greater collateral and lenders greater security. Assigning fixed carrying capacities achieved this, because the grazing permit itself could then be capitalized according to its net present value—that is, as the basis of an income stream of so many calves per year into the indefinite future. If a rancher defaulted, lenders could recover their losses by selling the permit on the open market. When a ranch changed hands, the same value could be part of the purchase price, underwritten by a mortgage.

The second assumption of early range research was simple reversibility: that damage done by excessive grazing would heal itself when grazing was reduced or eliminated. This seemed intuitively true, and the researchers' earliest experiences appeared to confirm it. The first thing they did was build fences to exclude livestock from their research plots, and soon they had photographs of striking fenceline contrasts: tall grass inside, almost no grass outside. It was as if fences themselves had the power to make grass grow. David Griffiths, the Santa Rita's first scientist, concluded that three years of complete rest would restore Southwestern rangelands to their original capacity. But complete rest was an impractical tool for the range as a whole—all those rancher-settlers would go bankrupt in that time, defeating the political purpose of the Western Range—so Griffiths and his colleagues set about calculating stocking rates that would permit grazing and recovery to proceed in tandem.

Some, including Griffiths, recorded observations that seemed to call the two assumptions, of carrying capacities and reversibility, into question. He noticed small mesquite trees beginning to establish in areas of grass, and he speculated that without fire they would continue to spread. The perennial grasses appeared to need back-to-back wet summers to germinate, an occurrence Griffiths witnessed only once in ten years. Different species of plants grew in different years, apparently due to the timing as well as the amount of rainfall. On top of this, cattle showed a remarkable ability to adjust their diets to prevailing conditions: they would eat annual or perennial grasses, brush, mesquite pods, even cactus if nothing else was present. Above all, the landscape was so varied over space and so variable over time that calculating static capacities was, in Griffiths's words, "a most difficult task."

These findings were out of step with those coming in from range research stations in other parts of the West, however. Where rainfall was greater or more reliable, fixed carrying capacities could be determined fairly easily and, when implemented, they produced demonstrable improvements in the range. In most of the West, moreover, the national forests were snowbound in winter and could only be grazed during the summer months. Because herds had to be moved onto and off of allotments every year, forest officials could impose "seasons of use." Herds could be kept off in the spring or removed mid-summer to give an allotment a period of time during the growing season to recover from grazing. In the Southwest, by contrast, most allotments could be grazed at any time of year, and continuous year-round grazing became the norm on most ranches as soon as perimeter fences were in place. Fencing was expensive, and in many cases only ranch boundaries—encompassing both private and leased lands—were fenced until late in the twentieth century. Although some prominent early researchers stressed the importance of rest periods for forage recovery, mechanisms for implementing this advice were lacking.

Why couldn't Southwestern rangelands be studied and administered differently from the rest of the West, to accommodate their unusual characteristics? Because both the U.S. Forest Service and the fledgling discipline of range science were intent on finding a universal knowledge of the range. The agency wanted it for ease of administration: uniformity in laws and policies and procedures throughout its large and growing system of national forests. Scientists wanted universality because that was the understood standard for any "mature" science: theories that explained all the available cases and models that could orient research anywhere.

Such a theory emerged from the Great Plains early in the twentieth century, when Frederic Clements of the University of Nebraska gave reversibility a theoretical foundation and a special name. He postulated a singular "climax community" of vegetation for any given site, determined by climate and soils. If disturbed—by drought or grazing or fire, for example—the site would pass through a series of intermediate communities on its way back to the climax. The series was both linear and fixed. Clements termed the process of advancing through it "succession."

During World War I another Nebraska student, Arthur Sampson, linked Clements's theory of succession to grazing and carrying capacities. Based on research in the Wasatch Mountains of Utah, Sampson conceived of

grazing as a counter-successional or retrogressive force, which pushed vegetation backwards along its linear series of potential communities. The more grazing, the further backwards it went; if grazing ceased, succession would return the vegetation to climax. In theory, one could balance the two forces and hold a range at a particular stage by adjusting the number of livestock and the season of use. After the war, Sampson left the Forest Service to become the nation's first professor of range science, and his theory became the central framework for range research and administration in the United States.

Thus, a model developed and refined elsewhere was adopted in the Southwest because it fit the scientific, political, and economic needs of the time. It was elegant in its simplicity, reducing the complex question of vegetation change to a single factor that any rancher, banker, or bureaucrat could understand: the number of livestock on a given amount of land. It appeared to explain short-term patterns observed by Griffiths and others: Following overgrazing, for example, perennial grasses were often replaced by annuals and unpalatable shrubs; when livestock were removed, perennials reasserted themselves. As for the longer term, for which observations did not yet exist, the Clements-Sampson model promised that no damage was permanent—that the land could always "heal" no matter how badly it had suffered—and this was no doubt reassuring for anyone contemplating the plight of Southwestern rangelands at the time. But it was precisely in the longer term that the limits of the model would be revealed.

OVERGRAZING AND FIRE SUPPRESSION

With the benefit of hindsight, it is clear that the idea of carrying capacity was tragically flawed in the Southwest. Observations at the Jornada Experimental Range reveal that annual forage production has been less than half the long-term average 50 percent of the time. Roughly speaking, this means that a stocking rate pegged for the "average" year will be 50 percent too high one year out of two—and probably 50 percent too low in the other. In extreme drought conditions, forage production can approach zero for an entire year. In short, there has never been a fixed number of livestock that a grazing allotment could support year after year.

Imposing carrying capacities dampened the highs and lows of the vicious cycle that had driven the Cattle Boom, but it didn't eliminate it altogether. During a wet spell, forage production would exceed what permitted numbers of livestock could consume, tempting ranchers to increase their numbers and making the official capacities seem needlessly restrictive. During drought, con-

versely, the grass fell short but the agencies could do little about it—after all, their own scientists had generated the capacity estimates on which the permitted numbers were based. It is no surprise that ranchers and agencies were perennially at odds over stocking rates.

The critical point is that during droughts, overgrazing could occur even if ranchers adhered to official stocking rates. Forest Service records from the Peloncillo Mountains suggest that actual stocking rates were generally in compliance with permitted numbers. Rangers did report cases of suspected overstocking, but such reports were the exception, not the rule. (No such records survive for BLM and state lands, where enforcement was

Sarah McDonald on shipping day, Sycamore Ranch. Her roots here go back six generations.

less robust and overstocking may have been more prevalent.) However, stocking rates were also remarkably stable over time, even as range conditions on many allotments oscillated up and down with rainfall. Rates dropped over the century in widely spaced steps, usually in connection with a permit changing hands. Rather than tracking the annual ups and downs of available forage, stocking decisions appear to have reflected longer-term changes in the ratio of grasses to shrubs.

In practice, then, the contradiction between good grazing management and fire prevention was resolved in favor of fire prevention, while the idea of fixed carrying capacities served to mask the contradiction in science and law. Stocking rates pegged to "average" conditions ensured that little grass would be present during severe droughts, thereby providing a built-in mechanism for reducing fire risks. Ranchers generally supported fire suppression as well, not least because early fences were built with flammable wooden posts. Forest officials did not explicitly endorse overgrazing as a means of fire prevention, and they may not have been able to compel stocking cuts during droughts in any case. Rather, the interests of ranchers, lenders, and bureaucrats aligned to favor stable stocking rates, which had the side effect of suppressing fires regardless of whether anyone consciously intended it. All the firefighters, tanker trucks, and aerial-suppression tactics deployed by the Forest Service were merely auxiliaries to this de facto fire suppression strategy. The outcome is clear from the tree ring record: large-scale fires virtually ceased after 1893.

Anywhere fires had once been common, their disappearance put grasses at a disadvantage relative to woody species. Conversion from grassland to scrubland or from savanna to forest took place at different rates and times depending on the site. Livestock could aid the process when, unable to find grass to eat, they devoured mesquite pods or cactus fruit and deposited seeds in nutrient-rich manure piles. Birds helped spread juniper berries, while rodents dispersed seeds from mesquite, oak, pine, and other species. Many shrubs and trees are vulnerable to fire in their seedling or juvenile years but can withstand it once they mature. Even twenty years without a fire, therefore, can result in qualitative and sometimes permanent change: low-elevation sites lose the capacity to carry a fire at all, because shrubs grow in patches surrounded by bare ground; higher elevation sites become so clogged with trees that fires will crown out, burning much hotter and more destructively than before. More than eight and a half million acres of Southwestern grasslands have been lost to this process, by one estimate, and many of them are effectively lost forever: A fire hot enough to burn through the shrubs would sterilize the soil and produce a moonscape. The area beyond this threshold steadily increases every year.

BATTLING BRUSH

The shortcomings of the Clementsian model became apparent to Southwestern ranchers and range researchers well before World War II, but for decades no alternative emerged to replace it. In 1937 scientists at the Santa Rita Experimental Range expressed surprise when they found that mesquite trees occupied nine million acres, or about three-quarters, of southeastern Arizona. Mesquite had clearly expanded from drainages out into the adjacent mesas and foothills, although it had not yet reached very high densities compared to what would happen in subsequent decades. Constrained by the conventional model, however, the scientists attributed the change entirely to cattle grazing and recommended lower stocking rates to address it. Eleven years later, surprise had turned to alarm. In an internal report on reauthorization of the Santa Rita and the Jornada Experimental Ranges, Kenneth Parker warned that mesquite and other woody species threatened not only the future of ranching in the region but the well-being of the watersheds on which growing cities and farmlands depended. He further

A crew of hotshots—wildfire-fighters—heads to work on a prescribed burn in the Peloncillo Mountains.

acknowledged that reducing or removing cattle would not stem the tide of brush encroachment. Instead of rethinking the conventional model's assumptions, however, Parker advocated finding ways of killing the shrubs outright. For the next twenty years the research agenda of the Santa Rita Experimental Range was dominated by pursuit of mechanical and chemical methods of brush control. (The research that gave birth to Agent Orange began with the quest to defoliate mesquite trees by aerial application of chemicals.) Hundreds of thousands of acres in the region were treated with bulldozers and chemicals between 1950 and 1980, but these tools proved both expensive and ineffective over the longer term: mesquites would resprout or recolonize in twenty years or less.

Until about 1980, the role of fire in Southwestern ecosystems was neglected by range science, if not altogether ignored. A handful of studies were performed by accident, when fires happened to burn across study sites set up for other purposes, but the issue failed to break into the mainstream of research. Only Robert Humphrey, an ecologist by training, attempted to build a career around studying fire, and he struggled to secure funding for his research program. He thus had to argue for fire restoration almost wholly on the basis of natural history, rather than in the more powerful language of controlled, replicable experimental findings. Other range scientists, meanwhile, responded that the issue of fire was moot because many sites no longer had enough grass to carry the flames anyway. Moreover, the Forest Service remained the single most important institution supporting range research, and the longstanding dogma of Smokey the Bear—rooted in "the traditional theory" that Aldo Leopold criticized back in 1924—was simply too strong.

Paradoxically, then, early research in the Southwest helped set the fledgling discipline of range science on a course that was not very well suited to Southwestern rangelands. Too many assumptions were imported from other places, imposed for reasons of political, economic, or scientific convenience. The result was a body of knowledge built around an incomplete model of arid and semiarid rangeland vegetation dynamics. It focused too narrowly on the short-term effects of different stocking rates, to the neglect of longer-term changes related to climate and fire, and it emphasized uniformity and averages instead of variability and extremes. Some range scientists recognized these problems, more or less explicitly and from early on, and over the decades they observed and recorded a variety of phenomena that simply didn't fit the model. But they lacked a theoretical framework to explain what they saw. The standard model was not easily displaced, meanwhile, because the institutions of the Western Range—leases, fences, grazing policies, and management practices—had been erected around it. Ranchers, bureaucrats, politicians, and many scientists had come to take the model's assumptions for granted, as would most environmentalists later.

In recent decades, the accumulated observations of Southwestern range scientists have helped force a major re-orientation in the discipline worldwide. Especially in arid and semiarid rangelands, "[v]egetation changes in response to grazing have often been found to be not continuous, not reversible, or not consistent." To accommodate this, alternative "state and transition" models have been developed, in which multiple factors interact in complex ways to produce changes that may be non-linear, irreversible, or context-specific: The effects of a fire, for example, may depend on whether it is followed by

drought or not. It is probably not a coincidence that state and transition models have been produced primarily by scientists working outside of the U.S. Efforts are under way to incorporate the new models into U.S. rangeland management, but it remains unclear how much the Western Range will have to change for this to work.

RAIN

Ranchers today have the peculiar habit of talking about rainfall in very small increments. Ask one, and you'll probably be told something like, "We got an inch and seventeen-hundredths at the house last week, but only forty-five-hundredths on the lease." Many of them can tell you the cumulative totals for the past year, for last summer or last winter, or for individual months, with separate figures for each rain gauge on their ranch. They can tell you how much it rained in the exceptionally wet winter of 1963 or the brutally dry year of 2002 (the driest single year, according to scientists, in the last fifteen centuries). If this seems an impossible act of memory, understand that ranchers also have a habit of talking about the rain all the time, etching each figure deeper into their minds. Most keep written records as well, and a few have been reporting their totals to the National Weather Service for fifty years or more as volunteer keepers of government weather stations.

This habit is the product of generations of learning, and it reflects the baffling variability of precipitation in the Southwest as well as its surpassing importance for range vegetation. If rainfall were reliably the same every year, such acts of monitoring and memory wouldn't be necessary. If it always fell at the same times of year, there would be no need to distinguish December from March, July from October. If it were uniform across the landscape, ranchers wouldn't have so many gauges, located sometimes no more than a mile or two apart. And if each drop were not so critical to the growth of plants, the precision of measuring to one-hundredth of an inch would be pedantic instead of practical. There is simply nothing reliable about rainfall in the Southwest, except perhaps that May and early June are almost always rainless and that a serious drought will occur once or twice in any ten-year period. You can calculate averages all you want, and you're likely to find that the average amount has never fallen in any actual month, season, or year.

The problem is not so much that rainfall is scarce overall, as it is in any semiarid zone, but that it varies so wildly over space and time. Monsoon rains are intense but highly localized: An inch or more may fall in a narrow path while adjacent areas remain completely dry. Bursts of abundant moisture can occur almost anywhere, at almost any time of year. The coefficient of variation—how far from the average a given year's total rainfall is likely to be—is greatest at lower elevations, where overall precipitation is lower, which means that the extremes are most pronounced where the vegetation is most vulnerable to disturbance. To make matters worse, variability in grass production is even greater than variability in rainfall,

Summer monsoon rainstorm on the Malpai Ranch. These downpours can cause severe flooding in some drainages but leave other ones nearby almost dry.

because how much the grass grows depends not only on the quantity of rain but also on when and how it falls. Different plants grow if it rains in the winter than if it rains in the summer. If it rains in late June or early July—the typical beginning of the monsoon—the perennial grasses germinate. But if it stops raining and is dry again for three or four weeks, most of the new plants die. Rain in October is too late for summer grasses, because temperatures aren't high enough anymore. An extremely light rain makes almost no difference, because it evaporates before the plants can make use of it. Conversely, a huge downpour may drop so much moisture so quickly that the soil cannot absorb it all and a lot is lost to run-off.

BILL McDONALD

The permittees mentioned in D. S. Marks's 1932 memo were Bill McDonald's ancestors. The family started ranching in the Peloncillo Mountains and the San Bernardino Valley in 1907, when five brothers—Buddy, Bill, Solomon, Alonzo, and Davis—brought their father, their families, and a herd of one hundred Hereford cattle across the valley from Silver Creek, north of Douglas. They established four homesteads in Cottonwood, Sycamore, and Guadalupe Canyons, and gradually they overcame John Slaughter's efforts to keep the southern Peloncillos to himself. Their combined operations grew to some 5,000 head of cattle before intergenerational succession pulled the ranches apart. (Two of Bill's closest neighbors—Drum Hadley and the Magoffins— live on old McDonald family ranches.) Today, just the Sycamore Canyon portion remains in the family, linked by leases to state land in the San Bernardino Valley and to national forest land in Cottonwood and Sycamore Canyons. The family has held the permit to graze the Cottonwood Allotment from its inception in 1910.

Bill is the fifth generation of McDonalds on the Sycamore Ranch. The ranching gene apparently skipped a generation, however: Bill grew up in Safford and Yuma while his father pursued a career teaching college English. He spent every summer on the ranch, and after earning a college degree in political science he moved there permanently to work under his grandfather, who passed away nine years later. The unusual succession gave Bill the reins in his mid-thirties, much younger than most ranch sons. It also meant he came to the ranch with wider experiences under his belt and something of a fresh perspective.

If Drum Hadley provided the vision for Malpai, and John Cook brought organizational resources and know-how, Bill has been its political helmsman, serving as executive director (or for a time, co-executive director) from the beginning. He is a tall man with large hands, an open face, and a gift for communication. Foundation officials, bureaucrats, donors, scientists, environmentalists, elected officials, and neighboring ranchers all seem comfortable talking to Bill to resolve differences and solve problems. "We'd gotten awfully good at knowing what we were against," he says, referring to the time before the Group formed, "and decided it was time to figure out what we were for."

The Cottonwood Allotment has an instructive history. Beginning in 1946, the permit was changed from year-round to seasonal use, November to July; in 1961 it was further restricted to November through April. The Forest Service supported the change because it meant that forage plants would be grazed only when they were dormant; they would have the summer growing season to recover. The allotment file consistently describes the McDonalds as conscientious managers; one ranger noted in 1942 that the Sycamore Allotment—which the McDonalds had acquired three years earlier and merged with the Cottonwood—"has made remarkable recovery since Mr. McDonald has been using it." Through the

Bill McDonald preparing to ship his cattle.

1950s, during the century's most severe drought, the family took "non use" of part of their permitted numbers almost every year. Conditions on the allotment were consistently described in Forest Service files as good, even during the drought.

The allotment illustrates several points. First, the timing of grazing is as important as the number of animals: Dormant-season grazing is much less damaging to plants than growing-season grazing. Second, overall numbers do matter, and reducing one's herd can help both cattle and grasses to survive a severe drought. Third, ranchers are constantly balancing grass and water supplies. Bill's grandfather probably supported seasonal use out of necessity as much as anything else: There wasn't enough water on the allotment to support his herd in the summer anyway, and he couldn't afford the artificial water investments that the forest rangers routinely recommended in their annual reports. By converting to seasonal use, he was able to stock more animals, but for a shorter period of time, such that the total number of "animal unit months" or AUMs—a standardized measure of forage consumed—did not change. The lower parts of the ranch, on state land in the San Bernardino Valley, were hotter in the summer than the allotment, but they were also flatter (making them easier for cattle to utilize) and able to capture more surface run-off in earthen tanks to support the herd.

Today, Bill sees variable surface water as a tool rather than a handicap, because it provides a way to control his cattle and maximize flexibility. He keeps careful track

Ed Roos manages Valley Mercantile in Animas, New Mexico. His ranch in the Peloncillo Mountains is covered by a conservation easement held by the Malpai Group.

of ephemeral pools in canyon bottoms, and he moves his cattle frequently. He knows he can graze certain areas only when water is available, and that when a pool dries up the cattle will go elsewhere and the nearby grass will rest. Some pools fill only one year out of five, some even less frequently. The system requires more time on horseback, but it costs much less than all the fences, wells, and waterlines that would be needed to impose a more uniform grazing capacity across space and time. It also imposes flexible but real limits on the impact his cattle can do to the range: They only graze in areas that have received enough rain to generate run-off, automatically avoiding the risk of compounding grazing and drought impacts.

Bill grew up believing the only good thing to do with a fire was fight it. As far as he knows, this was the view of all of his forebears as well. But when he moved to the ranch in 1975, he noticed that the grasses looked healthier in two areas of the Cottonwood Allotment that had burned in wildfires, one in 1961 and the other in 1972. By 1980 he was convinced that the allotment would benefit from a fire, but he didn't mention it to the Forest Service, figuring they'd veto the idea. Years later he learned that a biologist in the agency had recommended a fire in Cottonwood Basin at that time, but the district ranger had said nothing, figuring that Bill would veto it. A prescribed fire was finally implemented in 1997, as part of the Malpai Group's efforts.

——— ·—— ———

The Malpai Agenda called for a comprehensive scientific effort to monitor and study biotic change in the Borderlands, particularly in relation to livestock grazing. The logical place to begin such a program, one might think, was the field of range science. Yet the Malpai Group made a conscious decision to anchor its science program in the broader and institutionally distinct discipline of ecology instead. For years, environmentalists had dis-

David Dunagan placed a conservation easement on his family's ranch in the Animas Valley, where they have ranched since the nineteenth century.

missed range science as a shill for the livestock industry. More recently, and without recognizing the contradiction, critics of public lands grazing have found support for their views in the range science literature itself. Both arguments exaggerate and mislead, however. The problem with range science lay not in the answers it had produced but in the questions it had posed, or rather in the way it had had to pose them, given the constraints of the Western Range. It had good answers to old questions, and good new questions, but it did not have many answers to the questions being posed by the New West. No one did—hence the importance of both science and politics in the events that followed the Malpai Group's formation in 1994.

CHAPTER 4

THE RADICAL CENTER: SCIENCE, POLITICS, AND PARTNERSHIPS

From early 1993 into the following year, while the Malpai Borderlands Group was building itself into a formal organization, yet another battle over the Western Range was waged at the national level. The new Secretary of the Interior, Bruce Babbitt, launched an attempt to overhaul the administration of federal grazing lands and significantly raise grazing fees. The lines in the battle over "rangeland reform" were familiar, as was the outcome: The livestock industry fought "Cattle Free by '93" environmentalists to a standstill, producing piles of paperwork, bad feelings all around, and little in the way of actual changes. The two sides' positions were entrenched, irreconcilable, and alloyed with the larger ideologies of "left" and "right": government versus private property, regulation versus the market, nature preservation versus economic use. As in previous skirmishes, the battle tacitly endorsed the ecological assumptions built into the Western Range decades earlier: that livestock was the critical factor and that degraded

rangelands would repair themselves in proportion to reductions in stocking rates. From these premises, ranchers and environmentalists could only conclude that theirs was a zero-sum contest.

In deciding to form a nonprofit organization, the Malpai Group endeavored to define and promote an alternative position, which came to be called "the radical center." In their earlier discussions, they had come to consensus "that more government regulation was not going to help. At best,

it would replace one set of problems with another. The inevitable result of the free market would seem to be twenty-acre ranchettes. This was not the future we wanted to see for this land." Their position thus rejected both extremes and invited supporters from both sides of the debate—hence "center"—but it was not simply centrist. Rather than splitting the difference between two extremes, the radical center aimed to discard the polar oppositions that defined the spectrum in the first place. The challenge was similar to the one that the Hadleys and The Nature Conservancy had faced on the Gray Ranch—how to unite ranching and conservation, to make them complementary and symbiotic if not synonymous—except that the Malpai Group would have to confront it on an even larger and more complicated landscape. With three federal, two state, and more than two dozen private landowners, their effort would have to be public and multilateral. Criticism could be expected from both extremes, and the radical center might be stymied simply by the inertial resistance of the

Western Range, embedded as it was in a Byzantine system of rules, regulations, and habits.

The Malpai Group recognized that scientific knowledge and authority would be critical to making the radical center hold. Just as range science had helped to consolidate the Western Range, ecological science was now being wielded in the name of dismantling it. Malpai's position and proposals would have to be "radical" not simply in the sense of unorthodox or iconoclastic but in the literal sense of going to the roots of the matter, including the underlying ecological premises of the Western Range. The landscape had changed over the preceding century—that much was obvious, and a growing body of evidence indicated that simply removing livestock would not address many of those changes. But the relative importance of grazing, fire suppression, drought, and other factors to long-term vegetation change was not well understood, and it was even less clear what should be done now. What was driving ongoing brush encroachment? Were its current causes the same as its historical ones? Where, and to what extent, could grasses be brought back? What kinds of fires could do the job, if any? How were these questions related to other considerations such as biological diversity and endangered species?

Scientific research could shed light on these issues, but in most cases it would take years, even decades, to arrive at conclusive answers. In the meantime, much more than research alone was needed to overcome the political impasse between ranchers and environmentalists. As a voluntary, collaborative effort, the Malpai Group was committed to an approach that relied on persuasion rather than enforcement, agreement rather than rule. If only because of the public's stake in federal lands in the area, a "viable land ethic" had to be one that outsiders would recognize and endorse. In this regard, the process of scientific inquiry was as important as the findings. Critics of grazing were increasingly convinced that the ecological debate was over and that "the best science" was unequivocally on their side. To counter this view would require convincing people not only that many questions remained to be answered but also that the Malpai Group was genuinely interested in the answers— that they sought scientific research not to delay change or obfuscate matters but in order to achieve shared conservation goals. In short, Malpai needed to build trust, and trust rests on judgments of people rather than scientific knowledge. Through partnerships with scientists, agencies, and landowners, the Malpai Group built both a program of research and a growing network of supporters. Science and politics—often considered incompatible or mutually compromising—became reinforcing dimensions of the radical center.

RAY TURNER

Ray Turner provided the initial scientific perspective and guidance to the Malpai Group, participating in all but the earliest discussions. For nearly fifty years, most of them as an ecologist with the U.S. Geological Survey, he has studied Southwestern vegetation change at sites ranging from islands in the Sea of Cortez to high-elevation conifer forests in the Borderlands. Ray is best known for his use of repeat photography: comparing past and present vegetation by relocating the precise spots from which old photos were taken, taking new photos, and subjecting the pairs to detailed analysis. It is a somewhat unorthodox way to do ecology—compared to sampling plots or reading transects, for example—but in many ways it is as good as can be done given the circumstances. Plots and transects don't exist at all from before about 1910, and only in very limited numbers after that. Memoirs and newspaper accounts are older and more plentiful, but they tend to be vague and often subjective in their accounts of vegetation. Photographs have the virtue of being objective and repeatable, and if you can collect enough pairs you can begin to draw generalizations about regional patterns.

Ray's demeanor seems shaped by his chosen method: patient, diligent, affable, and calm. Tracking down old photographs that clearly depict landscapes is an archival endurance test, but it is nothing compared to relocating where they were taken. Few come with detailed annotations—at best they may mention a mountain range, a county, or a creek—and a ballpark approximation is not good enough. If the new photo is not exactly the same shot as the original, they aren't comparable, strictly speaking, and the whole effort is for naught. Ray is not satisfied until he stands on the very same spot, give or take a couple of feet at most, that the original photographer occupied decades before. Finding that spot is only possible at all because of the region's mountainous terrain and clear, dry air: Even early cameras could capture far-off ridgelines in detail, and by close examination of how topographical features line up in a photograph, one can triangulate the site very precisely. Not very quickly, however: Ray has probably spent years, in aggregate, pacing around the desert peering back and forth between the horizon and an old black and white photo. His camera, film, lenses, and technique are meticulously chosen to ensure that the new photo repeats the original as closely as possible.

Ray Turner at work, re-taking historical photographs of landscapes to measure long-term vegetation changes.

Ray's career reflects the challenges and uncertainties that afflict efforts to explain long-term, large-scale vegetation change in the Southwest. In 1965 he and his late colleague Rodney Hastings published *The Changing Mile*, an analysis based on several hundred pairs of photographs. It documented an upward shift in the elevation of major vegetation zones such as oak woodland, along with more obvious changes such as arroyo formation and mesquite encroachment. Sites that livestock could not reach—the bottoms of steep-sided craters, for example—displayed evidence of these changes as well, suggesting that some other cause than cattle had to be at work. Hastings and Turner rejected the hypothesis that fire suppression had driven the changes, mostly because they lacked solid evidence of the frequency of fires before 1893 (since found in tree rings) and secondarily because the condition of desert grassland and adjacent oak woodland sites prior to suppression seemed to require incompatible fire regimes. They concluded that grazing had contributed to vegetation change, but that "climate has to be accorded the more important role."

The Changing Mile is still viewed as a landmark in Southwestern ecology, both for its pioneering method and for its lasting influence on subsequent research. No one had brought such compelling evidence to bear on vegetation change over such a long time period and such

a large area. Hastings and Turner's conclusions have been carefully scrutinized and disputed, however, and Ray himself has modified his views significantly. In 2003, working with new collaborators, he updated the argument in *The Changing Mile Revisited*, based on sets of three photographs from each site. The effects of climate are reiterated in the new edition, especially in regards to arroyo formation, but fire is accorded much greater importance than before:

To sum up, reduced fire frequency is probably the primary reason why woody plants spread from watercourses onto adjacent grasslands after 1880. The open grasslands typical of earlier times were able to persist only as long as frequent fires acted on a fuel-rich landscape free of close-cropping herbivores. With the introduction of domestic livestock, reduction of fine fuel was combined with more efficient seed dispersal, simultaneously reducing the risk of fire and increasing the spread of woody plants.

Overall, Turner and his colleagues conclude that vegetation change has been driven by complex interactions among grazing, drought, and fire suppression, and that teasing apart the individual contribution of each is "virtually impossible." Whether shrub encroachment can be reversed probably depends on whether erosion has carried away too much topsoil at a given site to allow grasses to dominate again. They challenge advocates of restoration to "specify the ecosystem attributes that are to be restored" and to consider "how to maintain the processes that favored the original ecosystem attributes. For example, how could we possibly restore the Semidesert Grassland of our original photographs without periodic fires, and how could periodic fires occur in a landscape now subdivided into small housing tracts?"

Ray's influence on the Malpai Group may reside as much in his attitude as his expertise. He is deliberate, meticulous, and thorough in searching for "the best summary consistent with the evidence," and he is willing to change his views in light of new information, as can be seen by comparing the two editions of *The Changing Mile*. He considers ecological science not as a source of absolute or incontrovertible truth but as a means of gradually improving our understanding and knowledge. His stature and connections within ecology have proved valuable to the Group on numerous occasions, but his respect for evidence and method—for "letting the chips fall where they may"—has arguably been more important still.

ECOSYSTEM MANAGEMENT

Despite the stalemate and vitriol of the debate over rangeland reform, the early 1990s was an auspicious time for the Malpai Group to emerge. It was obvious, yet again, that federal legislation and top-down reform were unlikely to yield anything other than animosity and gridlock, and against this background Malpai stood out as a potentially more constructive way forward. Meetings of ranchers, land managers, wildlife officials, and environmentalists routinely degenerated into insulting tirades, whereas the Malpai discussions and subsequent get-togethers managed to remain civil and constructive. Bill McDonald and the Glenns both recall being inspired by the receptiveness they encountered among people who were concerned for Southwestern rangelands but not committed to either extreme in the debate. At the national level, meanwhile, Vice President Al Gore and Forest Service Chief Jack Ward Thomas were advocating an alternative approach that strongly resembled what the Malpai Group was proposing. It was called "ecosystem management," or sometimes simply "the ecosystem approach." Gore convened an Interagency Ecosystem Management Task Force in August 1993 to formulate recommendations for federal agencies. In their final report, released two years later, the task force featured the Malpai Group as a primary example and quoted Malpai members repeatedly.

High-level government support for ecosystem management helps explain why the agencies agreed so readily to programmatic cooperation with the Malpai Group at the meeting on the Gray Ranch in April 1993. But endorsing the *idea* of ecosystem management was easy, in part because no one really knew what it would look like in practice. It promised sustainability, prosperity, and social harmony—who could object to that? The Western Range had made similar promises, however, as had multiple use, sustained yield, and other "philosophies" for managing public lands. What made ecosystem management different? Broadly speaking, it resembled the vision behind the Conservancy's Last Great Places initiative: The subtitle of the Interagency Task Force report was "Healthy Ecosystems *and* Sustainable Economies." In the report, an ecosystem was defined as "an interconnected community of living things, including humans, and the physical environment within which they interact." Ecosystem management sought sustainability "through a natural resource management approach that is fully integrated with social and economic goals." In theory, ecosystem management would work at multiple scales, across jurisdictional and landownership boundaries, and it would use "the best science" to make collaborative management decisions. Sustainability would be measured not only in terms of products such as board-feet of timber or AUMs of grass but also in relation to ecological patterns and processes such as watershed function, species diversity, and disturbance regimes. The Malpai Group's mission statement, with its emphasis on "the natural processes that…support a diverse, flourishing community of human, plant and animal life," captured both the ambition and the orientation of this approach.

Rather than pretend to insulate science from politics, ecosystem management sought to integrate them by acknowledging the political dimension of natural resources and internalizing it, bringing interested parties of all kinds into the process of managing and studying ecosystems. The key premise of such an approach, philosophically speaking, is a presumption that what we don't know about ecosystems far exceeds what we do. Ecosystems are viewed as too dynamic, complex, and unpredictable to be controlled by humans, and any rigid management strategy is therefore expected to have counterproductive unintended consequences. The political implications of this premise are two: first, no one can claim to have infallible knowledge of what to do, no matter how technically skilled or powerful he or she might be; and second, everyone shares this predicament of uncertainty together. Science is stripped of omniscient pretensions, leaving a community of relative equals. The "right" answer is no longer understood as one that can't go wrong but rather as one that everyone can agree is worth trying, given the knowledge available. "Adaptive management"—from which ecosystem management is derived—stresses the importance of constantly reevaluating our knowledge and assumptions about ecosystems based on the results of previous actions.

THE SOUTHWESTERN BORDERLANDS ECOSYSTEM MANAGEMENT PROJECT

Late in 1993, the Forest Service issued a call for proposals to apply the principles of ecosystem management at pilot sites around the country. Building on the research already undertaken by the Conservancy in connection with the Gray Ranch, the Malpai Group teamed with scientists at the University of Arizona and the Rocky Mountain Research Station—a regional research arm of the Forest Service—to submit a proposal for a Southwestern Borderlands Ecosystem Management Project. The partnership of landowners, scientists, agencies, and the Conservancy was a feature that helped the proposal to succeed, securing about $400,000 per year for scientific research in the Borderlands.

The Coronado National Forest was a strong early supporter of the Malpai Group, and Forest Supervisor

Jim Abbott had assigned a senior range staff, Larry Allen, to work full-time with Malpai. The Soil Conservation Service (another agency of the U.S. Department of Agriculture, and now known as the Natural Resource Conservation Service) had made a similar commitment, assigning range conservationist Ron Bemis to a full-time position that was the first of its kind: no staff in the

agency had ever been authorized to work in two different states simultaneously. Larry and Ron had long experience working with the Malpai ranchers, and they were familiar with the regulatory and bureaucratic intricacies of their respective agencies. Along with Carl Edminster, a scientist with the Rocky Mountain Research Station, Larry and Ron became important advocates

Malpai Group advisors Larry Allen and Ron Bemis.

THE AUSTINS

Josiah and Valer Austin (pictured on page 98) are more than simply neighbors of the Malpai Borderlands Group. They own ranches to the west in the Chiricahua Mountains and to the south just across the Mexican border, and although they thus fall outside the primary planning area, they have been supporters, partners, and exemplars for the Group from its inception. On their El Coronado Ranch in the Chiricahuas, for example, the Austins have installed tens of thousands of small rock structures to combat erosion and improve the watershed, and they have collaborated with scientists and agencies to study and protect rare and endangered species such as the Chiricahua leopard frog and Sonoran mud turtle. By acquiring ranches along the border in Mexico, the Austins have helped to prevent development along the Malpai Group's southern border—where the challenges to conservation are different but no less serious than in the U.S.—and created important opportunities for cross-border cooperation, particularly in regard to scientific research and fire management.

and sources of expertise in developing a science program that was rigorous, relevant to practical issues, and administratively feasible. (The first bureaucratic problem they solved was about how to use federal research dollars on state and private land without violating the law.)

The Southwest Borderlands Ecosystem Management Project has completed cooperative projects addressing a wide range of issues. Researchers at the University of Arizona compiled a comprehensive bibliography of existing information about Borderlands natural history, containing some five thousand references. Scientists at the University of New Mexico used surveyors' field notes to reconstruct the dominant vegetation of the Malpai area at the time of settlement, one square mile at a time. They then compared the results to aerial and satellite images of present-day conditions to measure changes and identify patterns. The comparison confirmed a significant increase in shrubs in most of the area, correlated broadly with soil types. Another study expanded on previous research from the Tree Ring Laboratory of the University of Arizona to determine fire size and frequency throughout the region, going back more than five hundred years. The researchers concluded that before 1890, fires had swept across grassland valleys and up into higher elevations once every eight to twelve years. Other scientists found a similar pattern when they examined sediment cores from marshes on the Gray Ranch and elsewhere.

At the center of the research program were four experimental projects designed to address the major ecological processes affecting the Borderlands: fire, climate, and grazing. All were set up in the Malpai planning area, in hopes of producing results that would be directly applicable to the area. All were long-term studies, recognizing that a high degree of inter-annual variability limited the usefulness of experiments of less than five years' duration. Finally, all were launched in the midst of a severe and prolonged drought, which further constrained both the implementation and the interpretation of the research.

JIM BROWN

The most ambitious and complicated research project is a direct outgrowth of the work of Jim Brown, an ecologist at the University of New Mexico in Albuquerque. He is a past president of the Ecological Society of America and a prominent authority on Southwestern desert ecology, and his association with the Malpai Group represents another stroke of good fortune. In 1993, the Animas Foundation planned to endow a chair at the University of Arizona for a prominent ecologist working in the Borderlands, and Jim was one of the final candidates. He declined the position, which ultimately was not created at all, but his contact with the Malpai Group grew into an enduring personal and professional relationship.

In 1977, Jim established a long-term study site on fifty acres of land below Portal, Arizona, where the Chiricahua Mountains fan out into the San Simon Valley. He wanted to study the interactions of ants, birds, and rodents, and to do this he started by fencing the area against cattle. Then he divided the site into plots and fenced some of them in such a way as to obstruct the passage of rodents. In a subset of these plots he removed all the rodents to see what would happen without them. He gathered baseline data and found that the site contained fourteen species of rodents—more than are found in some entire states—and that it was dominated by grasses, with a scattering of mesquite and other shrubs.

Over the following decades, Jim and a series of graduate students and post-doctoral researchers observed dramatic changes in both the vegetation and the animal populations. Grasses declined significantly while shrubs took over the site. Concurrently, a dominant species of rodent—the banner-tailed kangaroo rat—declined and eventually disappeared altogether, while other species moved in or increased. The overall biomass of rodents and plants remained nearly the same, but their species compositions changed completely. The shift to shrub dominance was even more pronounced in plots where rodents had been removed.

When Jim and his students examined their climate data and compared it to historical records, they noticed a shift that appeared to explain what had happened. Beginning in the late 1970s and continuing for nearly twenty years, summer rainfall was somewhat below the long-term average while winter rainfall was several times higher. Conventional wisdom attributed shrub encroachment to livestock grazing and drought, which both tend to impact grasses disproportionately. But on Jim's study site conversion to shrubs had happened without cattle, during a period when overall annual rainfall was actually greater than normal. The loss of grasses could also be observed in grazed pastures surrounding the study site. It appeared that a change in the timing of precipitation—a relative increase in cool-season versus hot-season moisture—was sufficient to tip the competitive balance strongly in favor of shrubs, regardless of livestock. If anything, grazing—in this case by rodents—dampened these climatic effects.

McKINNEY FLATS

As a part of the Southwestern Borderlands Ecosystem Management Project, one of Jim Brown's former postdoctoral researchers, Charles Curtin, is conducting a study inspired in part by the research near Portal. On an 8,800-acre pasture of the Gray Ranch known as McKinney Flats, Charles is attempting to understand the interactions of fire, climate, livestock grazing, and various kinds of wildlife. Different combinations of prescribed fire and livestock grazing (neither, both, one or the other) are being applied to each of four parts of the pasture, and a wide range of data are being collected regarding vegetation, small mammals and herpetofauna (reptiles and amphibians), rainfall, temperature, and fire intensity. In addition, colonies of black-tailed prairie dogs, which were once common in the region but are now candidates for protection under the Endangered Species Act, have been reintroduced and incorporated into the study design. The project is supported by the Rocky Mountain Research Station, the Malpai Group, the Animas Foundation, and several other public and private sources, and it is designed to be at least ten years in duration.

Results from McKinney Flats are only provisional at this point but suggestive nonetheless. Vegetation dynamics appear to be driven much more strongly by rainfall (or lack thereof) than by any combination of fire and livestock grazing. Diversity of plants and animals is the same or higher in the presence of livestock than in areas fenced off from cattle, and prairie dogs appear to interact symbiotically with cattle by girdling shrubs and accelerating the cycling of nutrients, thereby inducing positive changes in grasses; the cattle are attracted to the grasses and in turn help keep them short, which helps the prairie dogs avoid predators. These findings, coupled with those from the site near Portal, led Jim and Charles to speculate that livestock grazing, like rodent herbivory, might actually dampen climatically induced shrub encroachment rather than accelerate it. To test this hypothesis they compared aerial photographs taken in 1946, 1957, 1976, and 1992 of a site in the Peloncillo Mountains, part of which was excluded from cattle since the late 1960s. Analysis revealed a two-fold increase in mesquite cover on the grazed side of the fence, compared to a six-fold increase on the ungrazed side.

BAKER I

The McKinney Flats project has been greatly facilitated by its location: on private land, under a single ownership, remote and isolated in a corner of the Gray Ranch. Two of the other three major projects in the Malpai science program also involve fire, but in the Peloncillo Mountains, where mixed landownership and federal law can make conducting prescribed burns far more difficult. In subsequent years, legal issues related to wildlife species protected under the Endangered Species Act would hamper implementation of fires (see Chapter 5). Leading up to the first large prescribed burn in 1995, however, the obstacles were of another kind: simple distrust among government biologists of Malpai's motives for burning at all. Baker I, as the fire came to be called,

illustrates the importance of the Malpai Group's partnerships in navigating the internal politics of land-management bureaucracies.

Conducting a large prescribed fire was a high priority from the beginning. It was envisioned as the first in a series of burns in the Peloncillos, with before-and-after vegetation monitoring conducted to evaluate effects on grasses and brush. How efficiently it could be done represented an important test of the cooperative agreement with state and federal agencies, who had acknowledged that their own lack of coordination was a major obstacle to fire restoration. A site was available in Baker Canyon, where Drum Hadley had excluded his cattle for a period of years to build up fuel. Part of the canyon was Coronado National Forest land, and Forest Supervisor Jim Abbott recognized the importance of moving quickly to demonstrate that the ecosystem management approach could yield concrete results. Numerous regulatory hurdles had to be cleared, however: the Bureau of Land Management and the Arizona State Land Department also had land in the area; part of the proposed burn area lay in New Mexico, meaning that both states' game and fish departments and BLM offices would have to be consulted; and the fire would overlap two Wilderness Study Areas, a federal designation that entailed greater review than would otherwise have been the case.

Two wildlife biologists, one with the Arizona Game and Fish Department and one in the Forest Service, raised objections to the fire in early 1994. Both observed that Baker Canyon was a tributary to Guadalupe Canyon, which was recognized as important wildlife habitat, especially for birds. One questioned the need for burning, saying that the area struck her as being in excellent condition already, with no significant brush problem and a great deal of grass. Whereas a "natural fire" would not be objectionable, a human-caused one, involving simultaneous ignition at multiple locations, ran the risk of burning so hot that it would "sterilize the soil, kill the grama grass, cause erosion, and eliminate food and cover for wildlife." She further questioned "the real purpose" of the fire, speculating that it was motivated simply by ranchers' desire for more forage for their livestock.

In a long memo, the other biologist raised similar concerns in much greater detail. Above all, he questioned the proposed timing of the fire, in late May or June, when summer temperatures and dry conditions could produce a very hot fire. This would magnify the fire's effects on vegetation and, in turn, on wildlife. He recommended burning in spring or fall instead, reducing the size of the burn and excluding it from sensitive sites such as riparian areas, steep slopes, and places with

Cattle and mule deer share habitat along Animas Creek on the Gray Ranch.

high fuel loads. Finally, he attached a list of five endangered, two threatened, and twenty-five candidate species of plants and animals that might be affected by the fire and thus raise legal issues under the Endangered Species Act.

The Malpai Group's partnerships were critical to addressing and allaying these concerns. Ron Bemis and Larry Allen led the effort from within their agencies, while the Animas Foundation and The Nature Conservancy assisted from the private sector side. In addition, a meeting was called at the Gray Ranch to gather the views of wildlife biologists, fire ecologists, and state and federal agency officials. Only five of twenty-seven attendees were ranchers, and the assembled ecological expertise made it impossible to question the quality of the review on scientific grounds. The key decision rested with Jim Abbott, who decided not to initiate formal consultation with the U.S. Fish and Wildlife Service regarding potential effects on endangered species (see Chapter 5). Planning was completed in only eight months, with ignition planned for June 1994. Because of the drought, however, wildfires kept popping up elsewhere in the region, drawing away the equipment and personnel needed for the prescribed burn. On June 26, a lightning strike set Sycamore Canyon on fire, putting the fire map to its first test. It failed: the BLM sent two air tankers to extinguish the fire even though it was in a "let burn" area. The Baker I fire finally took place one year later.

Scientific research has not yet resolved all the differences between ranchers and environmentalists, but it has redefined the debate in the Malpai Borderlands. Instead of a narrow focus on how many cattle are grazing on public lands, attention has turned to the complex interactions of climate, fire, grasses and brush, watersheds, and wildlife, as well as livestock. If not yet a matter of "verifiable facts," as envisioned by Jim Corbett, the conservation of the Malpai area has at least been recast as a set of interlocking questions, answers to which are slowly emerging from a suite of scientific experiments and studies.

In September 1994, the Rocky Mountain Forest and Range Experiment Station and the University of Arizona convened a conference in Tucson under the title "Biodiversity and Management of the Madrean Archipelago: The Sky Islands of Southwestern United States and Northwestern Mexico." Hundreds of scientists, government officials, land managers, and environmentalists from both sides of the border gathered for five days of panels, papers, poster sessions, and field trips. The conference proceedings, published the following July, ran nearly 700 pages in length. The Malpai Borderlands lie near the geographic center of the Madrean Archipelago, a 300-by-200-mile oval extending northwest beyond Tucson and southeast into the Sierra Madre. The Malpai Group had been in formal existence for less than a year, but it was at the center of the conference in other ways as well. In the plenary session, associate chief of the Forest Service David Unger called Malpai "an excellent example of the kind of collaboration that will be needed for successful ecosystem management." In a remarkably short period of time, the Malpai Group had attracted the support of federal agencies and credibility in the eyes of prominent ecologists. Bill McDonald delivered a short talk on "The Formation and History of the Malpai Borderlands Group," which he concluded by saying: "In a political climate where the traditional position on this issue of land use is usually to be at one end of the spectrum or the other, we find ourselves in the 'radical center.' We invite you to join us right there."

The Malpai Borderlands, according to Arizona and New Mexico Heritage Databases, is perhaps the most biologically diverse region in North America.

—Charles G. Curtin and James H. Brown, 2001

CHAPTER 5

BIODIVERSITY AND ENDANGERED SPECIES

The extraordinary biological diversity of the Malpai Borderlands is an accident of human and physical geography. The area happens to lie at the intersection of five biomes and to contain an unusually wide range of topographic relief, soil types, and climatic zones. Coupled with highly variable rainfall, these attributes have produced habitat for many organisms, but the area has been less than perfectly suited to intensive human uses. The permanent human population probably peaked between 1910 and 1930, when the last wave of hopeful ranchers and farmers homesteaded in the area, only to be forced out by withering drought and collapsing markets during the Great Depression. Without significant mineral deposits, the Borderlands could provide no viable living other than raising livestock, which could justify only minimal investments in altering the land to human purposes. Even when degradation of grasses and soils occurred, the land was not simplified in the manner of farms and

cities. If it stands out as exceptional today, part of the reason is that so much of the surrounding landscape did not share in this accidental good fortune.

There are at least two ways to try to apprehend and evaluate this diversity today. One is to consider those species of plants and animals that are found in the Malpai area but are otherwise rare: organisms with very limited ranges or that have suffered declines elsewhere, such that they are scarce by comparison to others within some larger geographical unit such as the world, the United States, or the states of Arizona or New Mexico. If these species can be identified and protected, then the overall diversity of the planet, the nation, or the states will be maintained. This is the perspective inscribed in law: There are thirteen species in the Malpai Borderlands that are protected under the federal Endangered Species Act, and dozens more have

been identified for special protection under state laws. The Southwest is one of the richest regions in the country for endangered species, and the Coronado National Forest has more of them than any other forest in the region. In some cases their rarity is absolute—the organisms exist only in very small numbers globally—but in others it is a consequence of the geographical scale of the laws: Some listed endangered species are common next door in Mexico, just as some species protected in New Mexico are abundant in Arizona (and vice-versa).

Alternatively, one can try to grasp the overall diversity of the area: the sheer variety of organisms found there, regardless of their rarity across larger areas or their well-being elsewhere in their ranges. There are an estimated 4,000 species of plants, 104 species of mammals, 295 species of birds, and 136 species of reptiles and amphibians in the northern Sierra Madre Occidental and the southern Apachian/Sky Island Complex, in addition to an unknown number of insects and bacteria. Taking this perspective is complicated, however, because it is clouded with uncertainties. The number of species in any given place is indeterminate: Even if we could isolate and study them all, the taxonomists would struggle to decide how to count them. As a practical matter, determining exactly what allows them all to persist is virtually impossible: What benefits some will almost inevitably harm others, after all. Hence the attractiveness of taking the first view, which narrows the focus of conservation efforts to what looks like a more manageable subset of biological diversity.

There are problems with the first view, however. One is that it ignores species until they are rare, by which time their prospects may already be seriously compromised. Waiting to act until a species has declined significantly makes the challenge of conserving it much more difficult. Behind this practical problem, moreover, lies a more fundamental one. If a species is very restricted geographically—as in the case of the Cochise pincushion cactus, for example, which is found only on a handful of limestone hills in the San Bernardino Valley—the single-species approach is fairly easy to translate into management prescriptions: The cactus can be monitored, mapped, and protected efficiently. But most species are not like the cactus. Instead, they are dispersed over larger areas, and they may move around. Such species are more difficult to inventory or monitor accurately; the threats, stresses, or limiting factors they face may be geographically distant and hard to isolate; they may move from one habitat to another seasonally or by life stage; and different populations may occupy dissimilar habitats, making it difficult to determine common habitat needs. At larger scales, then, the single-species approach faces rapidly increasing practical difficulties, and because biodiversity is ultimately a global metric, these problems challenge the coherence of the approach as a whole.

The Malpai Borderlands Group seeks to conserve a large area because its objectives—prevention of fragmentation, restoration of fire, remediation of shrub encroachment, and conservation of ranching as a livelihood—are more likely to be realized at the scale of the area as a whole than one property at a time. Its mission statement includes diversity, but it does not privilege rare species over common ones: "Our goal is to restore and maintain the natural processes that create and protect a healthy, unfragmented landscape to support a diverse, flourishing community of human, plant, and animal life in our borderlands region." If one does not prioritize species by rarity, and one cannot manage for them all one by one, then one must find another approach to conserving biodiversity. The Malpai mission statement does this by emphasizing the *processes* that sustain ecosystems, such as dispersal and reproduction, the cycling of water and nutrients through soils and plants, and disturbances such as fire, drought, frost, and flood. The interaction of these processes is complex, but the processes themselves are more easily defined and more limited in number than the organisms, habitats, or plant communities found in the area. Together, ecological processes produced both the organisms found in the area and their habitats, so one can presume that both common and rare species will persist if the processes are maintained.

In theory the two perspectives are complementary, but in practice they diverge. Malpai's mission statement resembles the first-named purpose of the Endangered Species Act: "to provide a means whereby the ecosystems upon which endangered species and threatened species depend may be conserved." For practical reasons, however, enforcement focuses not on ecosystems but on individuals of the listed species—products rather than processes. The law instructs the federal Fish and Wildlife Service to keep a list of threatened and endangered species and to protect them from "take," defined as "to harass, harm, pursue, hunt, shoot, wound, kill, trap, capture, or collect or to attempt to engage in any such conduct." "Harm" is defined to include "significant habitat modification or degradation," and the Fish and

Wildlife Service is required to define and designate "critical habitat" for each listed species, where regulatory oversight of human activities is augmented. But there is wide variation in how well habitats can be understood and managed for individual species, and if habitats are defined statically—by certain measures of vegetation type, cover, or structure, for example—it becomes difficult to incorporate the processes that produce them, because processes necessarily involve change.

In the Borderlands, the tension between a species- and a process-based approach is greatest in relation to fire. Restoring periodic burning may be a means of preserving habitat for listed species—it may indeed be necessary—but such effects will be long-term and indirect.

From a legal perspective, by contrast, what is most relevant is the possibility of direct or immediate effects. A fire that kills an individual of a listed species constitutes "take" regardless of long-term benefits to the species as a whole, whereas activities that have no direct effect on listed individuals (e.g., fire suppression) do not constitute take even if their indirect effects may be significantly detrimental. The Fish and Wildlife Service must somehow resolve these trade-offs and potential contradictions.

Neither approach is foolproof, and there is no incontrovertible general argument for favoring one to the exclusion of the other. The Malpai Group "trusts the processes," so to speak, to create conditions favorable to all of the organisms that evolved in the area. The Fish

Douglas High School students participating in Chiricahua leopard frog propagation and restoration efforts, San Bernardino National Wildlife Refuge.

and Wildlife Service protects species judged to be at risk of extinction by shielding extant individuals from direct or foreseeable harm. The tensions between these competing approaches to biodiversity conservation have been revealed by four species in particular: the Chiricahua leopard frog (*Rana chiricahuensis*), the jaguar (*Pantera onca*), the lesser long-nosed bat (*Leptonycteris curasoae yerbabuenae*), and the New Mexico ridgenose rattlesnake (*Crotalus willardi obscurus*). Two are wide-ranging whereas the other two occupy small, discrete locations; two have proved tractable by collaboration with scientists whereas the others have not; and two have obstructed the Malpai Group's attempts to restore an ecological process—fire—whereas the others have not. Comparing them thus affords a chance to evaluate whether and how the two approaches can be combined in practice.

THE CHIRICAHUA LEOPARD FROG

The formation of the Malpai Group in 1994 occurred at an auspicious moment relative to the fate of the Chiricahua leopard frog. In the preceding five years, herpetologists had conclusively documented a sharp decline in occurrences of the species, which had once been found at more than eighty sites in southeastern and east-central Arizona. Neither cattle grazing nor fire were considered major culprits in this decline: The principal threats to the leopard frog were non-native predators (bullfrogs and numerous fish species) and a poorly understood fungal disease called chytridiomycosis. Although listing under the Endangered Species Act was widely considered to be inevitable, the species was not yet formally protected; it gained protection under Arizona state law in 1996 and was federally listed as threatened in 2002. This meant that for a period of years the scientific community was more engaged with the frog than the federal regulatory community, and that management activities for the frog could therefore proceed with less red tape than would be the case later.

Ranchers Matt and Anna Magoffin set the tone for Malpai's leopard frog activities by hauling thousands of gallons of water by truck, week after week for more than two years, to sustain a population in a stock tank that was drying out during the drought. Scientists were unaware of the population's existence, and the tank was on private land. The Magoffins could easily—and legally—have allowed the frogs to perish. But Matt worked at the neighboring San Bernardino National Wildlife Refuge, where scientists were observing the frog's decline with some dismay. He invited them to the ranch to see the frogs in the tank. Both the fungus and the non-native predators were absent there. Needless to say, the scientists were thrilled.

By sharing the news of the stock tank population, going to such lengths to sustain it, and engaging the scientific community directly, Matt and Anna set in motion a process of building trust and cooperation around the then-novel idea that private ranchers could help preserve endangered wildlife. The Magoffins, the Malpai Group, and the herpetologists went on to develop a captive breeding program in partnership with the Douglas public schools, establish a population in another tank on the Magoffins' ranch, and obtain funds to drill a well and install a separate mini-tank for the frogs. The "win-win" arrangement—by which leopard frogs, cattle, and ranchers all obtained benefits from the same water development—was subsequently codified in Fish and Wildlife Service rulings, becoming the template for leopard frog conservation efforts throughout the region.

Although less ideal than natural streams as frog habitat, stock tanks have two major advantages at the present time: first, they reliably have water in them, whereas many natural streams have dried up in the past 120 years; second, their isolation makes it more likely that bullfrogs and other non-native predators can be removed or have not arrived at all (the same might be said for disease, although the details of chytridiomycosis are not yet fully understood). In some areas where natural waters never existed, herpetologists believe ranchers' stock tanks once enabled leopard frogs to expand their range, until non-native predators such as the bullfrog arrived later in the twentieth century. In recognition of these facts, the listing of the leopard frog expressly exempted normal use and maintenance of stock tanks from the Endangered Species Act's take prohibitions. This "section 4(d) rule" reflects the judgment that even if leopard frogs are harmed or killed by cattle using a stock tank or by a rancher maintaining a stock tank, the stock tank's value as man-made habitat presumptively outweighs these harms.

As formal listing of the leopard frog approached, the Malpai Group decided to take a further step. The 4(d) rule only discouraged elimination of frogs from stock tanks; it did nothing to *encourage* ranchers to allow their tanks to become refugia for frogs. To rectify this, the Malpai Group worked with the Fish and Wildlife Service to develop a legal mechanism, known as a Safe Harbor Agreement, that extends a similar level of indemnification to ranchers who intentionally create habitat or introduce frogs to existing habitat. Prior to such actions, surveys are conducted to measure frog populations at a site; any frogs subsequently found above this "baseline" figure are excluded from legal protections. In an unprecedented acknowledgement of the Magoffins' earlier, pre-listing efforts in behalf of the frog, the Fish and Wildlife Service assigned a baseline of zero to their ranch. The Chiricahua Leopard Frog Safe Harbor Agreement was signed in 2004.

THE JAGUAR

Like the leopard frog, the jaguar was not yet protected under federal law when it first became an issue in the

Malpai Borderlands. In March 1996, Warner Glenn encountered a large male in the Peloncillo Mountains in the course of his work as a professional hunting guide. Jaguars had been documented in Arizona sporadically in the past, and in 1972 the species had been listed as endangered from the U.S.-Mexico border south (its range extends all the way to Argentina). But this listing did not apply to jaguars north of the border, apparently due to a paperwork foul-up that had occurred in the mid-1970s. The Fish and Wildlife Service had pledged in 1979 to rectify the error "as quickly as possible," and in 1994 it published a proposal to extend the listing to the United States. The proposal stalled, however, for lack of proof that any such jaguars still existed. The last confirmed sighting dated to 1986, and no breeding animals had been found in the U.S. since 1910. The nearest core habitat was about two hundred miles to the south, in the Sierra Madre of Mexico, whence individual animals, usually young males, occasionally made their way north.

Warner had been hunting mountain lions in the region for more than fifty years, from the age of eight. His father, Marvin, bought his first hunting dog in 1937 and learned the trade to stem the tide of calves and colts killed by lions on his ranch in the Chiricahua

The jaguar Warner Glenn encountered in the Peloncillo Mountains.

Mountains. Eleven years later he took his first paying client, and he and Warner soon became a father-and-son team, hiring out to hunters during the winter and tracking down lions from livestock kills for area ranchers year-round. They often wondered about jaguars, and in the 1970s they made two trips into Mexico to hunt them, but they never found one. Marvin passed away in 1991, by which time the family business had passed into Warner's hands, assisted by his daughter Kelly. Five years before Marvin's death, when a jaguar was shot in the Dos Cabezas Mountains near his ranch, Marvin and Warner had talked about whether they would still want a trophy if the opportunity presented itself. They had decided no—they wouldn't shoot it unless they had tracked it directly off of a dead calf. Ten years later, when the opportunity did arise, Warner reached only for his camera. He shot nineteen photos, many of them from less than ten feet away and without using the viewfinder, while the cat snarled and his dogs kept it at bay. Then he called off the dogs and the jaguar departed.

Thirteen of the photographs turned out—the first ever taken of a live, wild jaguar in the U.S. Warner had proof to back up his story, but reasons to hesitate telling it at all: His sighting could lead to the jaguar being listed as endangered, which might result in restrictions on cattle grazing and lion hunting in the Peloncillo Mountains, or even on federal lands throughout the region. His dream of seeing a jaguar, now realized, might end up threatening his and his family's two livelihoods and lifelong activities. He hadn't shot, so there was no need to shovel, but there were still reasons to shut up.

Warner called Bill McDonald, both for advice and because the encounter had occurred on the Sycamore Allotment. Bill suggested that he call John Cook. John recommended inviting all the agencies to come to the Malpai Ranch to see the photos and hear the story. "I don't see that it could do any harm," he said, according to Warner's recollection. When Warner went public it became national news. The *New York Times* printed a story with one of his photos. Requests poured in for interviews and copies of the photographs. Twenty-eight agency personnel showed up for the meeting.

Six months later another jaguar was encountered in the U.S., on a ranch in the Baboquivari Mountains near the Buenos Aires National Wildlife Refuge. (It too was found by lion hunters, who videotaped it sitting in a tree.) The species would soon be listed throughout its range under the Endangered Species Act, and the Fish and Wildlife Service had to decide what would and would not constitute "take" under the listing. Should the jaguar's rediscovery in the Borderlands be seen as evidence that current land-management practices were working to conserve the species, as the Malpai Group maintained, or as grounds for curtailing currently permitted activities? The Arizona Game and Fish Department convened a Jaguar Conservation Team to gather input and information, and a long series of large and frequently tense public meetings ensued. Environmentalists pressed for restrictions on hunting with dogs and on grazing, and for designation of critical habitat in the U.S. A species so rare, they argued, called for the utmost precaution.

The Malpai Group's response combined science, politics, and economics. They invited Alan Rabinowitz, one of the world's leading jaguar biologists, to tour the area and evaluate habitat conditions in the U.S. and Mexico. He concluded that the U.S. was on the fringe of the jaguar's range, without suitable habitat to support a breeding, resident population. In his judgment, the fact that individual animals wandered into the U.S. did not make the U.S. critical to the survival of the species. To cope with demands for photos and interviews, Warner decided to publish a short book about the encounter, with ten of the photos, his own first-person account, and short essays by Ray Turner and Jay Dusard, a local photographer and author. In case a jaguar killed any livestock, the Malpai Group established a fund to reimburse ranchers for their losses; a portion of the proceeds from the book was dedicated to the fund. Finally, to cope with the persistent acrimony afflicting the conservation team, Malpai invited Jamie Clark, national head of endangered species issues for the Fish and Wildlife Service, to visit and tour the area.

The result was rules that Malpai could live with: lion hunting and livestock grazing could continue, and no U.S. critical habitat was designated. Penalties for shooting a jaguar increased significantly, and hunters were henceforth required to notify officials of any sightings. Since then, a monitoring program using trip-photography has been implemented to document jaguars in the Peloncillos and other mountain ranges further west. More jaguars have been sighted in this way in recent years, although not in the Peloncillos. Controversy continues to surround the jaguar, however, and some environmental groups have filed suit to force designation of critical habitat in the U.S.

THE LESSER LONG-NOSED BAT

The lesser long-nosed bat is a migratory, nectar-feeding species listed as endangered in 1988. Surveys conducted in the mid-1980s led the Fish and Wildlife Service to conclude that the bat had declined dramatically in southern Arizona since 1940, and the listing speculated that this posed a threat not only to the bat but also to several cactus species (e.g., saguaro and organ pipe) for which it serves as a pollinator. Were the bat to disappear altogether, "the future of the entire southwestern desert ecosystems" might be imperiled, according to the official listing. Since that time, both the decline in numbers and its possible ramifications have been called into question by leading bat biologists, and populations are now believed to be stable or increasing. But at the time the Malpai Group was founded, scientists and environmentalists were concerned that the availability of

Palmer's agave (*Agave palmeri*), whose flowers are a major food source for the bat in late spring and summer, might be limiting the bats' reproduction and survival. This in turn raised concerns about fire and livestock grazing. Agave flowers are found at the tops of tall stalks, which each plant produces once before dying. Fire can kill agaves, and cattle (as well as numerous wildlife species) can prevent flowering by browsing the stalks when they are bolting. In August 1990, for example, one scientist found that twenty out of thirty-eight bolting agaves at San Luis Pass on the Gray Ranch had been eaten off between 0.4 and 1.2 meters above ground. Whether these impacts could in turn affect the bat was unknown.

When planning the Baker I fire in the Peloncillo Mountains, the Forest Service chose not to consult formally with the Fish and Wildlife Service (see Chapter 4). This decision allowed the fire to proceed quickly, but it also entailed some legal risks: The Forest Service could be accused of skirting the letter of the law. When planning began for the Maverick fire, in 1996, presumption had changed: the Forest Service requested formal consultation regarding possible impacts on the lesser long-nosed bat, the Mexican long-tongued bat (another nectar-feeder), and the New Mexico ridgenose rattlesnake. (Eight other listed species were also evaluated, but the Fish and Wildlife Service concurred with the Forest Service's determinations, meaning that formal consultation was not required for those species.) A series of letters, site visits, phone calls, and meetings ensued between March 1996 and March 1997, involving representatives from the Forest Service, the Fish and Wildlife Service, the Arizona and New Mexico Game and Fish Departments, the Natural Resource Conservation Service, the Malpai Group, and The Nature Conservancy.

In January 1997, the Malpai Group convened a meeting of twenty-three ecologists, biologists, and agency representatives to discuss the complex of issues surrounding fire, agaves, and nectar-feeding bats. This meeting was crucial for several reasons. First, it brought together virtually all the known experts on the topics in question: grassland ecologists, bat specialists, fire specialists, agave specialists, and range conservationists from agencies, nonprofit organizations, universities, and research institutions. Second, the assembled expertise agreed that very little scientific information existed to address the specific issue raised by the Maverick fire: would it hurt the bats by hurting the agaves? Third, they also agreed on several more discrete points: that very few bats occurred in the Peloncillo Mountains; that larger numbers were known from within twenty miles of the proposed site (and therefore within foraging distance); and that the short-term and long-term effects of a single fire on agaves were probably minimal. Fourth, the group was then able to formulate specific research

Peter Warren, Malpai Coordinator for The Nature Conservancy.

questions: Does fire kill agaves? Does it have other effects on agaves, via germination or competition from grasses? Are agaves a limiting resource for the bats? Finally, the Rocky Mountain Research Station agreed to support research into these questions through its Southwestern Ecosystem Management Project.

The Malpai Group and its partners did not contest the new presumption against fire vis-à-vis listed species, nor did they claim to be able to meet the burden of proof it entailed. Instead, they turned the situation on its head: No one could meet a burden of proof one way or the other, because there wasn't sufficiently specific information. The clear need thus became to get such information, whatever it turned out to be. Blocking the fire no longer looked prudently cautious but needlessly stubborn; the Fish and Wildlife Service could instead authorize it as a necessary experiment and opportunity to learn. In a memo summarizing a follow-up meeting two weeks later, the Conservancy's full-time Malpai coordinator, Peter Warren, wrote: "We don't have answers to all the concerns that have been raised, but we all agreed that the only way to get the answers is to do some burning and use the opportunity to conduct monitoring and research so we can learn from it and adapt our fire program in the future." Less than two months later, the Fish and Wildlife Service issued a Biological Opinion authorizing incidental take provided that mortality of burned agaves did not exceed 20 percent.

Scientific research subsequently indicated that fire did not pose a threat to agaves or to the bat. A study was conducted to evaluate the effects of the Maverick fire and another, accidental fire on the Gray Ranch on the reproduction of agaves. The study found less than 4 percent fire-related mortality and no effect on nectar and pollen production. It also suggested that fire may increase germination and establishment, resulting in a longer-term benefit to agaves. The more fundamental question—whether the bat is food-limited in the region—remained unanswered until 2000, when a student at the University of Arizona studied the bat's foraging ecology and analyzed population data on both bats and agaves. She found there were five to twenty times as many agaves as the bats needed, depending on annual fluctuations in flowering. As a direct result of this research, the lesser long-nosed bat no longer poses an obstacle to prescribed fires in the region.

THE NEW MEXICO RIDGENOSE RATTLESNAKE

The Malpai Group launched a similar effort regarding the New Mexico ridgenose rattlesnake. Experts from various agencies, nonprofit organizations, and universities were assembled and consulted; site visits took place to examine habitat and discuss fire prescriptions; plans were put in place to study the fire's effects on the rattlesnake and its habitat. But the outcome was quite different: Instead of resolving tensions surrounding the rattlesnake, as it did with the bat, the Maverick fire actually made them worse.

The rattlesnake is found in only three disjunct locations: the Sierra San Luis in Mexico, the Animas Mountains of the Gray Ranch, and the Peloncillo Mountains. It inhabits rocky wash bottoms with abundant plant litter and an overstory of trees. The Peloncillo population is by far the smallest—too small to permit replicated experiments or statistically meaningful sampling. The Sierra San Luis population is by far the largest. Perhaps coincidentally, the incidence of fire in the three ranges loosely correlates with snake abundance: the Sierra San Luis has experienced the least fire suppression and the Peloncillos the most. The Peloncillos habitat is so different from the

New Mexico ridgenose rattlesnake.

other two sites, however—lower (and non-overlapping) in elevation, for instance—that fire suppression may have had opposite effects there. (The name Peloncillo derives from the Spanish for "bald," suggesting that the range may have had almost no trees circa 1800.)

The incidental take statement for the Maverick fire permitted up to two direct mortalities and two instances of harm via habitat alteration, and it mandated measures to rescue and relocate snakes encountered during the fire. It also required the fire to take place during the dry season (i.e., before monsoon rains began) when the snakes were most likely to be underground and out of harm's way. None of these terms were violated when the fire occurred in late June 1997.

In conjunction with the fire, a study was conducted to evaluate direct and indirect effects on montane rattlesnakes. Nine snakes (including three ridgenose) were radiotagged and monitored before, during, and after the burn. Only one (a rock rattlesnake) perished in the fire, and behavior was not strongly affected: frequency of movement declined, but rebounded once the rains began; other parameters were unchanged or inconsistent. These findings might have allayed fears and cemented a consensus in support of prescribed fires in the Peloncillos, but for two things. First, the fire escaped its primary boundaries and burned very hot in Whitmire Canyon, one of five known occupied ridgenose rattlesnake habitats in the Peloncillos. Second, the snake that perished was the only one located in an area of high fuel loads. Whether the flames in Whitmire Canyon killed any ridgenose rattlesnakes was unknown, but they coalesced with the dead rock rattlesnake to produce a theory among some snake biologists: Fires might be more intense than in the past due to fuel buildup from decades of fire suppression, and crown fires might destroy the trees and thereby the rattlesnake's habitat. In writing up the results of the study, the biologists urged that "artificially high fuel loads" be reduced "prior to reintroduction of large-scale summer fires."

The empirical evidence for the biologists' theory is tenuous. Two out of three radiotagged ridgenose rattlesnakes survived a crown fire in the Sierra San Luis in 1989; the third was not found. Much of the research on the subspecies has been conducted in an area of the Animas Mountains that also experienced a stand-replacing fire that year. Even the snake biologists acknowledge that fires of some kind are inevitable in the long term, and that prescribed fires are an effective way to reduce the probability of catastrophic burns. After conceding these points, the biologists nevertheless speculated that "fire-induced changes in the environment" might result in behavioral shifts that could affect the persistence of the species. The study could neither prove nor disprove their theory—indeed, their theory could not be tested experimentally at all because the Peloncillo population is too small and habitat conditions in the other ranges are too different.

Given this scientific-evidentiary impasse, it soon became clear that the more critical factor was trust among the various stakeholders. Efforts to craft a programmatic fire plan for the Peloncillos, and a plan for the next prescribed fire, Baker II, bogged down in recriminations and suspicions of bad faith. The snake biologists began to suspect that the Malpai Group's only motive for fire restoration was to produce more grass for cattle, regardless of larger ecological considerations. They also began to distrust the Forest Service's claims that other means of fuels reduction would be prohibitively expensive. The Fish and Wildlife Service's lead snake biologist, Jim Rorabaugh, wrote to his supervisors in April 2001 to object to the removal of terms and conditions he had recommended for Baker II and the programmatic plan. In his memo, he complained that "the Coronado and Malpai are trying to exclude" dissenting biologists from the process, and that "the Forest has not been honest with us about what they can or cannot do to protect the snake and its habitat." He complained further that

PRESCRIBED AND NATURAL FIRES IN THE MALPAI BORDERLANDS

Fires have occurred on approximately 312,130 acres (nearly 488 square miles) of the Malpai Borderlands since 1989. A small portion of this total is attributable to accidental, human-caused fires or to burns conducted for research purposes on McKinney Flats and elsewhere on the Gray Ranch. The vast majority, however, falls into two categories: prescribed fires and natural fires.

It is important to understand that the total acreage is measured as the area within the fire perimeters, not the amount of ground actually burned. No fire burns evenly across the landscape, and every fire leaves behind a mosaic of burned and unburned areas; some areas burn very hot, consuming virtually all above-ground vegetation, while others burn less intensely, leaving larger trees scarred but not severely damaged.

The three prescribed fires conducted in the Peloncillo Mountains under the Malpai Borderlands Group fire program account for only 20 percent of the total: Baker I burned 6,000 acres in 1995; Maverick burned 9,014 acres in 1997, and Baker II burned 46,458 acres in 2003. Each required significant planning and coordination between state and federal agencies and private landowners to agree on a prescription—that is, conditions of temperature, humidity, wind speed and direction, fuel loads, and fuel moisture levels under which the fire could be set, as well as ignition and containment strategies. Because of severe drought, large wildfires elsewhere in the West, and Endangered Species Act considerations, it took six years to arrive at a prescription for the Baker II fire. The fire itself cost $124,467 to conduct, or about $2.68 per acre. The Malpai Borderlands Group paid $20,000 of this.

Meanwhile, some 250,000 acres have burned on the Gray Ranch, at an estimated cost of only $1.25 per acre. Under an agreement between the Animas Foundation and the New Mexico State Forester's Office, natural fires (caused by lightning) are handled on a "least-cost suppression" basis, meaning that they are allowed to burn themselves out within broadly spaced firebreaks (roads and washes, in most cases). This strategy is possible because of the unique combination of lcircumstances there: single ownership, predominantly private land, isolation from human habitations, and a fifty-year history of relatively frequent fires that have kept the vegetation resilient to burning. Moreover, because the fires are not set by humans, they do not raise liability issues under the Endangered Species Act.

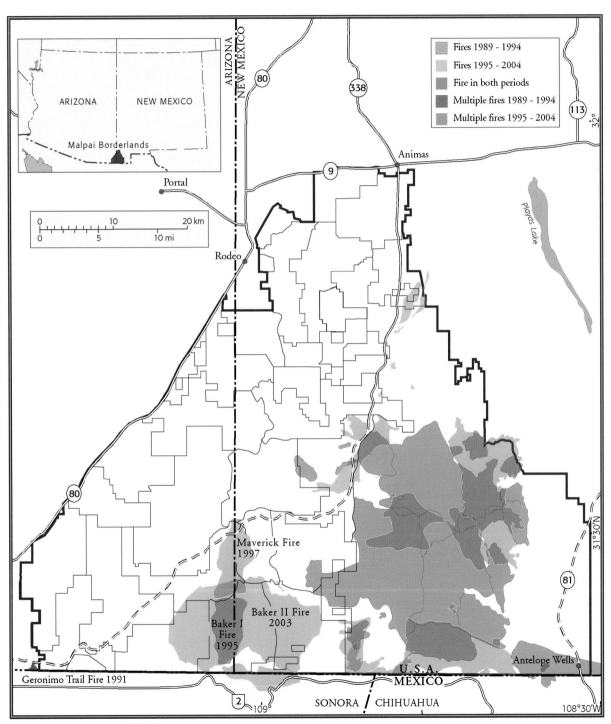

Legend:
- Fires 1989 - 1994
- Fires 1995 - 2004
- Fire in both periods
- Multiple fires 1989 - 1994
- Multiple fires 1995 - 2004

ARIZONA   NEW MEXICO

Malpai Borderlands

Portal

Rodeo

Animas

Playas Lake

Maverick Fire 1997

Baker II Fire 2003

Baker I Fire 1995

Geronimo Trail Fire 1991

Antelope Wells

U.S.A.
MEXICO

SONORA / CHIHUAHUA

Map 3: Fire in the Malpai Borderlands

the biological opinions for Maverick, Baker II, and the programmatic fire plan all lacked the teeth necessary to hold the Forest Service to its commitments regarding the rattlesnake. Another biologist later explained that the removal of Rorabaugh's terms and conditions had caused him to begin to distrust Malpai's influence and integrity.

On the other side, members of the Malpai Group concluded that the aggrieved biologists were taking out their frustrations in other spheres, in collusion with Rorabaugh and other Fish and Wildlife Service staff. Their chief evidence was language inserted into a biological opinion regulating livestock grazing on Bureau of Land Management lands in southern Arizona. The insertions, made after a draft had circulated for public comment, became part of the final ruling without any opportunity for review by the Malpai Group or other affected parties. The language effectively prohibited prescribed fires on any BLM land above five thousand feet elevation in the Peloncillos, even though very little such land existed (most BLM parcels are lower) and even though no ridgenose rattlesnakes had ever been found on BLM land. As an official Fish and Wildlife Service ruling, this language automatically became the baseline for future rulings on other federal lands, and because the affected parcels are scattered amidst Forest Service lands, it had the potential to stop prescribed fires throughout the Peloncillos. The rationale given for the ruling relied heavily on the published work and unpublished opinions of Andrew Holycross, one of the dissenting biologists whom Rorabaugh felt had been "disinvited" from Malpai meetings and research.

Simply stated, the process of building consensus through ecosystem management broke down over the rattlesnake, and the cost of the breakdown was delay. After numerous rewrites of fire plans, draft biological opinions, and an expensive habitat mapping effort, the Baker II fire was ignited in June 2003—six years after the Maverick fire and more than five years after planning had begun. It served as a test of provisions contained in a draft programmatic fire plan for the Peloncillos, under which specified percentages of ranked snake habitat units would be permitted to burn at high intensities. Covering 46,458 acres of private, BLM, national forest, and Arizona State lands, the Baker II fire is reportedly the largest prescribed fire ever conducted successfully in the western United States. Preliminary analysis indicates the fire did not exceed the permitted 20 percent threshold of high-intensity fire in potential rattlesnake habitat. Research projects on the rattlesnake are again being implemented, this time with a partially new group of biologists.

PRESUMPTION, RISK, AND TRUST

The four species examined in this chapter reveal the importance of presumption, risk, and trust for any attempt to integrate the species- and process-based approaches to biodiversity conservation. If a management activity is presumed to be benign to listed species—as in the case of the Baker I fire, for example—then the burden of proof falls on the Fish and Wildlife Service to demonstrate otherwise—by finding a dead individual after the fire, for instance. If presumption is against an activity, on the other hand, then the burden of proof falls on those proposing it to demonstrate that it can be done in such a way as to spare the species from harm, or at least from existential jeopardy. The Endangered Species Act does not stipulate where presumption lies in general, and in practice it is the subject of maneuvering both within and between government agencies. The Forest Service claimed presumption in the case of Baker I but could not do the same for Maverick; biologists responded to Maverick by inserting a de facto presumption against fire into the biological opinion regarding livestock grazing on BLM lands. The 4(d) rule, the Safe Harbor Agreement, and the zero baseline for the Magoffin ranch all represent formalizations of presumption in favor of ranching-related activities at stock tanks vis-à-vis leopard frogs.

In our society, it is widely believed that nature will take care of itself if humans do not disrupt or disturb it—meaning that in debates about conservation, presumption favors inaction and the burden of proof falls on those proposing an action to demonstrate its benefits ahead of time. There are two problems with this standard. First, inaction isn't necessarily possible. Bullfrogs and chytrid fungus will continue to decimate leopard frog populations if humans do not intervene, and catastrophic wildfires will become more common if fuel loads are not actively managed. Taking no action is, effectively, acting to let these things happen. Second, demonstrating the benefits of a management activity ahead of time may be impossible, at least in the strong sense of demonstration as statistically significant, predictive scientific findings. If the jaguar listing had banned lion hunting, it would have eliminated the very activity that had made it possible to discover that jaguars were present in the U.S. again.

Two categories of risk can be distinguished in these cases, although they are often conflated: the legal risk of taking an action that results in "take," and the more general risk of taking an action with uncertain or unpredictable consequences. The Malpai experience suggests both the importance and the difficulties of addressing the

Anna, Chris, and Matt Magoffin. The Magoffins initiated the Malpai Group's efforts to protect the Chiricahua leopard frog, and subsequently placed a conservation easement on their ranch.

second category of risk. Executing the Maverick burn required building a consensus among diverse experts to act despite uncertainty about how the fire might affect endangered species. The Fish and Wildlife Service permitted the burn—addressing the first kind of risk—in the name of learning more about these potential effects and thus reducing the second kind of risk. Scientific methods were a crucial means of satisfying everyone that such learning would occur. Regarding agaves and the lesser long-nosed bat, this approach worked: significant findings satisfied everyone that fire did not pose a threat. But the same standard backfired in the case of the ridgenose rattlesnake. Precisely because the findings were statistically inconclusive, room remained for divergent interpretations and heightened differences of opinions about fire.

The rattlesnake case exposes the degree to which management activities and endangered species conservation do not—and cannot—rest on science alone. Choosing statistical significance as the sole measure of certainty only heightens the sense of risk at those inevitable moments when such significance cannot be obtained. The Malpai Group's success in addressing the leopard frog was built not on scientific findings but on interpersonal relationships and actions of all sorts: sharing the existence of the Magoffin ranch population with scientists and agency officials, and hauling water to sustain it even when it was not yet legally protected and many landowners would have happily allowed it to perish. Likewise, the success of the meeting of bat, fire, and agave experts presupposed their belief that the Malpai Group would in fact allow the scientific findings to shape subsequent fire planning—a belief strengthened by the prior history with the frog. If trust is required to overcome the second kind of risk—to act in the face of uncertainty—then it is plain that trust depends only in part on science, regardless of the strength or weakness of its findings. In the rattlesnake case, trust evaporated when people perceived others as acting surreptitiously, and the loss manifested in counteractions in other arenas, such as the BLM biological opinion. Trust is multi-dimensional: it attaches to individuals or groups as agents responsible for all of their actions, not simply those directly related to the issue at hand.

———

The Malpai Group and its agency partners have devoted countless hours of effort to resolve the issues raised by endangered species in the Borderlands, particularly in relation to fire. These were significant legal issues that required real work to address. But ecologically speaking, the tension between a species- and a process-based approach to biodiversity conservation turns out to be more apparent than real. It results from mistakenly thinking that all species can be understood and managed along the same lines as those few, like the pincushion cactus, that are discrete and extremely limited geographically. In other words, the uncertainty and risk associated with a process-based approach are not unique to it. Science has not yet come close to producing predictive knowledge about what it will take to conserve the vast majority of species, and it is vain to think that such research will be completed any time soon. This is not to say that research is irrelevant—the lesser long-nosed bat case clearly demonstrates otherwise—but rather that scientific findings are ultimately less important than one might think. More decisive for the Malpai Group's achievements has been their ability and willingness to act *both* on the basis of scientific findings *and* when such findings are incomplete, inconclusive, or unobtainable, recognizing that trust, rather than certainty, will be the standard ultimately employed to judge those actions.

A site on the Gray Ranch following a fire. In foreground, an agave cactus, a principal food source for the lesser long-nosed bat. Beyond that, mesquite trees that were top-killed by the fire.

These magnificent hillside lots present a rare opportunity to own property in this undisturbed scenic area. Building sites with breathtaking views of Cave Creek Canyon, the Chiricahua Mountains, Portal and the Rodeo Valley. Borders State land, BLM and the Coronado National Forest with an array of distinctive desert vegetation. Nature abounds where the desert meets the mountains on these unique parcels.

—Real estate listing,
Hatch Realty Southwest, Rodeo, New Mexico

CHAPTER 6

The Specter of Subdivision

Subdivision is the specter that gives urgency to the mission of the Malpai Borderlands Group. Opposition to it was the most basic point of agreement in their early discussions, one thing that the ranchers and the environmentalists whole-heartedly shared. For both ecological and economic reasons, subdivision represents a threshold change, irreversible and irremediable. "Show me an over-grazed ranch—I can work with that. We can do something about it," says Ron Bemis, Malpai

Coordinator for the Natural Resource Conservation Service until his recent retirement. "But once that ranch is paved over, there's nothing we can do." The social and cultural ramifications are no less stark: Like the tourists once envisioned on the proposed Animas National Wildlife Refuge, the residents of subdivided ranches—exurban "ranchet-teers"—seem incompatible with local ranchers' sense of themselves, their community, and the landscape they share. On all these dimensions, more-over, subdivision has a self-reinforcing dynamic that

spreads across property boundaries: When one ranch converts, the odds rise for those next door. Ranching becomes more difficult, land values rise further, and the temptation grows to sell out and move. Fire restoration becomes effectively impossible, not only on the developed parcels but also on adjacent state and federal lands, and as grasses gradually decline agricultural productivity and profitability dwindle, exacerbating the pressure to convert to another land use.

When the Malpai Group first formed, many outsiders believed the risk of subdivision there was small: It was too far from any big city to become a bedroom community, and none of the towns nearby was booming. Some even suggested that Malpai was overreacting. Today, in a time of nationwide real estate speculation that has rural homesites in southeastern Arizona appreciating 10 to 20 percent annually, the Malpai Group appears to have acted in the nick of time. There is a mini-boom taking place on the northwest edge of the planning area, from Rodeo, New Mexico, up into the Chiricahua Mountains around Portal, Arizona, and similar development can be found in almost every valley in the region. By one estimate, roughly half of all the private land in Arizona—more than six million acres—has been subdivided in the last half-century. Many of those parcels are still large by urban standards—twenty or forty acres, for instance—and many do not yet have houses on them. But they are much too small for livestock production, and once they have been capitalized at development values no herd can possibly pay for them.

Remarkably, the Malpai Group may well succeed in preventing subdivision from invading its planning area. Of the roughly 468,000 acres of private land there, 310,760 acres are now covered by conservation easements that prevent subdivision—two-thirds of the readily developable land. The Nature Conservancy holds an easement on 235,000 acres of the Gray Ranch, while the Malpai Group holds easements on twelve other ranches with a total of 75,760 acres of private land. Another 134,620 acres of state and federal land are linked by leases to these ranches, meaning that 56 percent of the entire Malpai Borderlands is affected, directly or indirectly, by the easements. An unfragmented future is by no means guaranteed, but it is far more likely than in any comparable area in the region. How this has been achieved, its complexities and qualifications, and the ecological consequences of subdivision are the subjects of this chapter.

PROPERTY: PUBLIC AND PRIVATE, RIGHTS AND VALUES

In their struggle with environmentalists over the Western Range, ranchers have often cast their position in terms of defending property rights. Their rights in private land (and water), they argue, are threatened by various environmental regulations, from county zoning ordinances to federal pollution statutes. Meanwhile, their leases to graze on public lands should be recognized, they say, as property rights as well. On this view, cuts in stocking levels on leased lands amount to a form of "takings" that require compensation under the Constitution. The most vociferous critics of the Malpai Group from the "right" end of the political spectrum subscribe to these arguments.

The intermixture of private, state, and federal landownership on Western ranches does raise important issues—the point of the Western Range, after all, was to link public and private lands together into viable ranch units—but these issues are more accurately understood in terms of property values than rights. The courts have

repeatedly found that leases to graze livestock on federal lands confer privileges, not rights. What is really at stake if stocking is reduced is the market value of the lease itself: How much it contributes to the sale price of the ranch. This value is capitalized in ranch purchases; ranchers may borrow against it; they may pay property taxes on it—in these respects leases do resemble private property. Moreover, a cut in a lease can affect the profitability of the entire ranch, perhaps rendering it nonviable. But what is at risk is the value of a rancher's investment.

Similarly with regulations on private lands: What someone will pay for a ranch depends on what can be done with it, and for ranches today the potential for residential development generally accounts for 50 to 90 percent of their market price. If that potential is eliminated by government action, in theory the value of the ranch will drop accordingly. It is not hard to understand why ranch owners would resist such actions—it is no different, really, from suburban homeowners defending their property values.

A conservation easement allows a ranch owner to be compensated for the development potential of his or her private land at current market values. The terms of the easement can be negotiated like any contract, allowing the parties to adapt provisions to suit the specific circumstances of the land and people involved. The price of the easement is determined by subtracting the appraised value of the ranch with the easement from the appraised value without it. Once executed, the easement is recorded as an encumbrance on the title, and it "runs with the land"—that is, it remains in effect regardless of changes in ownership. The entity that holds the easement is legally obligated to enforce it, which in extreme circumstances may involve taking legal action.

Conservation easements were first used in the U.S. in areas dominated by private land (generally the Northeast), and their use in the Western Range setting is

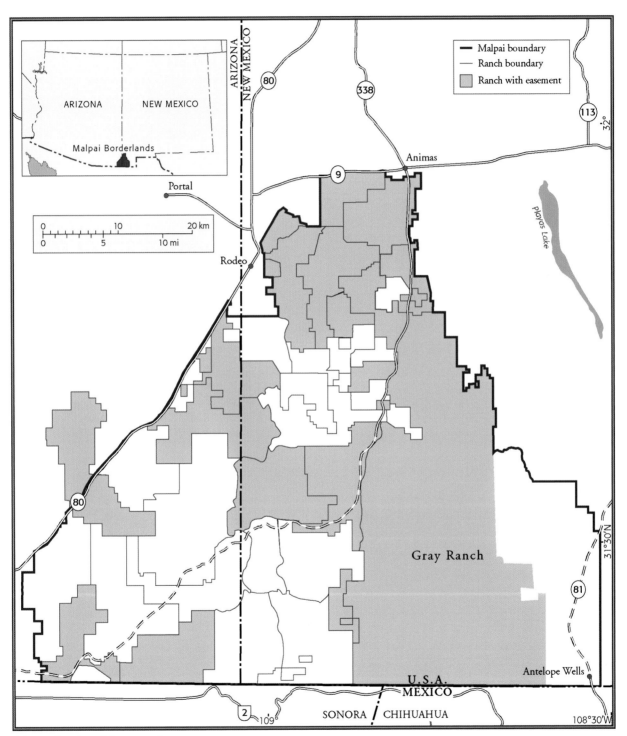

Map 4: Ranches with conservation easements

complicated by ranchers' dependence on leased land. What if a ranch's private land base is too small to support a viable livestock operation, as is generally the case in the Southwest? If there is a conservation easement on the private land, and leasehold is lost, the remaining property would have value neither for livestock production nor for development. This scenario would once have seemed improbable, because state and federal leases were presumptively renewable on ten-year terms. But recent decades have seen this presumption eroded by legal and political challenges from environmental groups (and to a lesser degree recreational interests), such that the possibility of severe cuts or termination of grazing leases is now quite real. For some ranchers conservation easements are not an option for this reason.

GRASSBANKING

In November 1992, in a talk at the University of Arizona, Drum Hadley publicly proposed the idea of "grassbanking" for the first time. Ranchers needed to rest their pastures for two to five years to build up fuel for fires and to recover after burning, but most ranchers couldn't afford to sell their cattle and then buy new ones later. During severe drought, they might need to move their cattle regardless of fire, to protect their animals as well as their range. Instead of leasing other range for cash, Drum asked, what if ranchers could obtain grass by exchanging the development potential of their private lands? What if grass could become a currency for conservation? Negotiations with the Conservancy over the Gray Ranch, which were ongoing and still secret when Drum spoke, demonstrated that the portion of a ranch's market value attributable to its development potential was substantial, and that it could be realized through a conservation easement. Why not exchange development rights for an equivalent value in grass? Drum reasoned that like money in a bank, grass compounds over time: the more you have, the more it produces. Over the

preceding century, this fundamental asset had been depleted; now it was time to reinvest, to build it back up. A grassbank could help do this while simultaneously preventing subdivision.

The Gray Ranch was an obvious place to try it: It had the grass, and unlike federal lands it was not subject to complex restrictions on sub-leasing. Leveraging conservation on surrounding ranches fit squarely into the mission of the new Animas Foundation. Two years later, four ranchers from the Animas-Rodeo area began moving their herds onto the Gray, and in January 1996 they placed easements on their private ranch lands, totaling 17,400 acres. The value of the easements translated into

Drum Hadley.

Billy Darnell, one of the original grassbank ranchers, and his daughter, Danielle Lasher, providing supplemental feed to their cattle during the winter breeding season.

three to five years of grass for their herds. The Malpai Group became the holder of the easements and raised funds to reimburse the Animas Foundation for the value of the grass it provided. Like the leopard frogs on the Magoffin Ranch, this "win-win" outcome for ranching and conservation made good copy, and the grassbank was prominently featured in *Smithsonian* magazine and the *Los Angeles Times*. The idea has subsequently caught on elsewhere, with more than twenty grassbanks now operating or in formation across the West, and the term is sufficiently catchy that the Malpai Group decided to trademark it in response to signs that it was being diluted or abused—used as a way of marketing "conservation" in connection with developing homesites, for

example. Curiously, meanwhile, the Gray Ranch grassbank has not had any further participants: Since the Malpai Group learned it could successfully raise funds for easements, ranchers have preferred the flexibility of payments in cash. Nevertheless, the grassbank served the crucial purpose of demonstrating that easements could work in the Borderlands.

The circumstances that made the grassbank work were unusual and specific to the area: the Animas Foundation owning the Gray Ranch, with even more grass than usual due to reduced stocking since 1990, is only the most obvious one. The searing drought of the time is another, since it put local ranchers in need of grass for their cows. (The drought persisted through 2003—if indeed it's over yet—and it may partially explain subsequent easement sales as well.) A third critical circumstance was the legal expertise and creativity of Mike Dennis, the Conservancy attorney who has helped craft all of the easements in the Malpai area. Brainstorming with the Malpai Group, he came up with a simple, novel solution to the problem posed by state and federal grazing leases: a clause whereby the easement may be released if a ranch loses its grazing privileges "independent of any action taken by the parties" to the easement—due to changes in laws or policies, for example. (Release is not automatic, but subject to "mutual consent" of the rancher and the Malpai Group.) The federal and state agencies that own these lands remain ultimate arbiters of their use, but the contingency comes close to creating the kind of "mutually binding obligation" between private landowners and public agencies described in the original Malpai Agenda. It provides, bluntly speaking, an unprecedented form of leverage for lessees: If an agency chooses to cancel a lease (or if an environmental group sues to terminate grazing on leased land), it does so at the risk of reopening the ranch's private lands to subdivision and development. (The clause also means that the easements do not meet IRS requirements for conservation-related charitable donations, but the ranchers involved didn't need tax deductions anyhow, especially during the drought.)

Perhaps the most important circumstance, however, was that the ranchers in the area were willing to participate at all. Easements were not yet widely known or understood in the Southwest, and they were anathema to many property rights advocates vocal in the ranching community. That the grassbank ranchers were nonetheless receptive is attributable to a series of events that had begun some fifteen years earlier, when a ranch just south of Rodeo was bought by a developer and divided into forty-acre lots. Before long another ranch nearby did the same, and then another. As large grazing properties, the land was worth only $50 to $100 per acre; as homesites it was selling for $400 to $800 per acre. The Rodeo-Portal corridor was falling to subdivision like a line of dominos.

The four grassbank ranchers are neighbors who witnessed these changes firsthand; one of them is the son of the man whose ranch had been the first domino. Their houses are scattered along the base of the Peloncillo Mountains from Rodeo around to Animas, and they share fences up in the hills behind. They did not jointly decide to put easements on their ranches. Rather, they looked at their options, they looked at Rodeo, and they each made the same decision. Together, their decisions ensured that subdivision would not creep around the north end of the Peloncillos and into the Animas Valley.

For Edward Elbrock it was an easy decision for a number of rather particular reasons. He was recently divorced, and his only heir was dating a man who had repeatedly encouraged him to subdivide the ranch. He himself had partaken briefly in the subdivision wave, when he resold some lots he had purchased at tax auction, and it had left him with something of a guilty conscience. In addition to the ranch, Edward has a heavy-equipment business that has flourished from the local boom by drilling wells, installing septic tanks, dozing sites for foundations, and blading dirt roads. He's not proud of his role in development, but he figures someone else would do the work anyway if he demurred. All of these factors made him want to keep subdivision out of the Animas area, where he has lived all his life. When the grassbank came along, he had already decided he wanted to put an easement on his ranch, but he hadn't been able to interest The Nature Conservancy's New Mexico chapter. He contacted Drum when the Animas Foundation bought the Gray, hoping to lease some grazing there. The grassbank fit his needs perfectly. "I'm glad not to be tempted to subdivide," he says now.

As part of the grassbank agreement, the Malpai Group conducted monitoring on all four ranches, using the same protocol that the Animas Foundation employs on the Gray Ranch. The objective was to document the effects of resting the ranches from livestock grazing. In general, sites that were already in fairly good shape responded to the rest—these tended to be at higher elevations, with greater average precipitation and more grass to begin with. But there was so little rain in the years 1995-1998 that the grasses had minimal opportunity to grow even without livestock, and lower, drier sites that were in poor condition showed little response or even degraded further for lack of moisture.

Despite the mixed results, the grassbank experience was a positive one, according to Mary Winkler, a grass-banker whose ranch house looks directly out over Rodeo. She says the monitoring taught her a lot about the grasses on her ranch, and that removing the cattle helped her recognize both the seriousness of the drought and the sensitivity of the land. Only in the third year on the grassbank did she begin to see improvement in the grasses on her home ranch. She and her husband, Rich, cut the herd substantially when they returned from the grassbank, and they have changed their management to stock more conservatively and rotate pastures to provide rest periods for the grasses.

Likewise for Edward Elbrock. He measured less than twelve inches of rain in the first three years his cattle were

Grassbankers Tricia and Edward Elbrock with some of Tricia's prize-winning ewes and lambs.

Grassbankers Mary Winkler and Wart Walter at a former homestead on the Winklers' ranch. The Malpai Group helped coordinate with the NRCS and the BLM to develop a water system that serves both the Winklers' and the Walters' ranches, improving livestock distribution in a remote area of the Peloncillo Mountains.

away, and he chose to stay off for a fourth year rather than risk returning too soon. He says things would have been even worse had he not used the grassbank. More generally, he reports that being part of the Malpai Group has improved his relations with the BLM, which owns much of the land his cattle graze. Edward has learned not to expect rapid responses in the vegetation. As late as 1962 his ranch was sufficiently free of shrubs and trees that his family could cut three hundred tons of native grass hay. He has watched juniper trees gradually invade his pastures over the past thirty years, and more recently the drought has killed about 20 percent of them. As a kind of experiment, he fenced off a forty-acre area on his ranch where the grasses had disappeared. Today the site is about 80 percent recovered, he says—nearly forty years later.

The Malpai Group has completed an average of one easement per year since 1997. Some details vary, but the core provisions are basically the same in all of them. The Malpai mission statement is recited as the general intent of the easement, and ranching and hunting activities are expressly permitted. Subdivision, dumping, pollution of water, and intentional conversion to non-native vegetation are prohibited. A baseline report on current conditions is completed at the Malpai Group's expense within six months of execution of the contract, and the easement prohibits human-caused degradation of the range and its wildlife from this baseline. (Degradation due to climatic factors such as drought is exempted.) The easements do not stipulate how this goal is to be achieved, other than to say that livestock production activities "are to be carried out according to the best standards of ranching historically practiced within the region of MBG at the time of its incorporation, and to the conservation practices encouraged by MBG." All ranch and grazing management authority remains with the ranch owner. As explained in a newsletter from 2001, "Our easements are written to preclude subdivision of ranches and perpetuate open spaces. They are not written to manage ranching."

Patience has been the cardinal principle of the Malpai Group's approach to easements. They have never made a list of properties they aspire to protect, nor have they solicited easements from landowners. They have a policy not to put peoples' names on the maps they generate, and ranches whose owners don't want to be associated with Malpai are designated "not applicable." There is no need to advertise in their community: Word gets around, and even the skeptical neighbors have observed carefully. With time, ranchers who were aloof from the Malpai Group have become participants, and a few who were once openly critical have come forward to sell easements. Malpai stands ready to discuss an easement with any landowner who approaches them, on a simple first-come, first-served basis, and they have yet to say no to anyone—although several deals have had to wait while funds were raised. "This country rewards perseverance," Bill McDonald remarks, "and not a whole lot else."

LINKING ACROSS SCALES

Conservation easements have been possible because of the links the Malpai Group has forged between local landowners and a more diffuse, national community of philanthropic foundations and donors. For locals the important issues are daily and tangible ones: what the landscape looks like and how it is used, who their neighbors are, what their children and grandchildren will experience as they grow older. For some, deciding to take an easement may be the only way through tight financial straits. For foundations and donors, by contrast, the issues are generally larger in scale and more abstract in conception: conservation of biodiversity, wildlife corridors, and habitat, or the preservation of a culture or a livelihood. This disparity is an inevitable consequence of the scale and location of their respective circumstances. There is no intrinsic reason why the two communities shouldn't connect, the locals becoming a concrete realization of the outsiders' goals and ideals. But they are unlikely to find each other and work together without someone serving as a kind of translator, explaining and representing each to the other. This is the work that the Malpai Group has excelled in doing, and they have done it, in large measure, by bringing individuals from the philanthropic world into the Malpai community and developing relationships with them—relationships that all parties view as genuinely meaningful. The process began when Drum brought John Cook to the Malpai Ranch for the fire meeting in March 1993, and it has expanded ever since.

A coatamundi, photographed by a remote trip camera installed to detect jaguars.

WARNER AND WENDY GLENN

The Malpai Group's office was originally installed in a bedroom in Warner and Wendy Glenn's house. Their ranch was centrally located—to the extent that any place can be in such an enormous, relatively roadless area—and they had more bedrooms than their neighbors. When they bought the ranch as newlyweds, in 1960, it had no house. But the nearby Slaughter Ranch—originally Ignacio Ortiz's Rancho San Bernardino—was in the midst of a development scheme, and the developers allowed the young couple to live temporarily on the property until the surrounding lots were sold. "Six months to a year," they were told

it would take. Seven years later the scheme had evaporated—homesites are hard to sell without electricity—and Warner and Wendy moved into a trailer on their own place. This became their headquarters, where they subsequently built a home to accommodate their hunter-clients as well as their family.

Appropriately enough, the Malpai Ranch house has since become dual-purpose, devoted equally to hunters and to the Malpai Borderlands Group. A large, two-story wing has been added to accommodate the office, and a patio has been enclosed to create a large second dining room. Malpai Group meetings routinely draw fifty people or more, and the Glenns' kitchen serves lunch for

Wendy and Warner Glenn on the Malpai Ranch.

them all. Meals are preceded by a blessing, and the food is abundant and Southwestern ranch-style: beef, beans, rice, squash, tortillas, salad, and dessert. Western paraphernalia occupies every wall and corner: spurs, historical maps, old pieces of barbed wire, a life-sized poster of John Wayne (and numerous smaller ones of Kelly Glenn-Kimbro, long-time spokeswoman and model for Ruger firearms). Photos of lions, hunters, cattle, mules, hounds, and family abound, and a giant blowup of Warner's best jaguar shot overlooks the original dining room. Another large room serves as "the museum," where Warner and Wendy display an astonishing collection of prehistoric artifacts, fossils, frontier-era tools, wildlife skulls, and archaic firearms. The hallways are lined with long shelves of books on Southwestern history, archaeology, art, food, and literature.

From a distance it would be easy to stereotype the Glenns as Western clichés, but it doesn't work for anyone who's spent more than five minutes in person with them. They are at once archetypes of Western lore, heritage, hospitality, and skills, *and* thoroughly original, dynamic, and forward-thinking. Somehow they harness the values and symbolic potency of the Old West to move in an entirely new direction. Prior to the Malpai Group's formation, they were openly critical of the Conservancy and environmentalists, defensive of private property rights, and suspicious of scientists. But they silently agreed with environmentalists' successful campaign to end the bounty on mountain lions—a battle in the late 1960s that set the tone for future confrontations with the cattlegrowers—and the entrenched bitterness of the rangeland conflict eventually struck them as self-defeating. John Cook, Mike Dennis, and other Conservancy staff displayed a more positive, constructive outlook that appealed to the Glenns. The criticism they fielded from ranchers in the early days of the Malpai Group actually reinforced their determination, because so many of the accusations were untrue.

The Glenns have hosted hundreds of visitors for the Malpai Group: donors and foundation officials, politicians and bureaucrats, curious well-wishers and suspicious critics, accomplished scientists and wide-eyed graduate students, journalists and film-makers, and conservation groups from throughout the world. Warner and Wendy insist that they have learned more from all these visitors than the visitors have learned from them, although they also admit that their hospitality is itself a kind of pedagogy. "People will come a long ways to look if somebody will take the time to show them," Warner points out, but they don't learn much if they stay at the nearest hotel, in Douglas. In their offices, bureaucrats tend to be defensive and detached from the land. "Reality sets in when they get out here." Bill McDonald puts it slightly differently: "We've found that the agencies have a lot more latitude to do things than they let on, if you can get them in a comfort zone where they feel you've got common goals… You begin to have less interest in labels and more interest in individuals." For most visitors, the Malpai Ranch is where they find this comfort zone, where "outsiders" and "insiders" become members of the same community.

More than two dozen private institutions have supported the Malpai Group, including numerous family foundations, state and national cattlemen's foundations, wildlife and conservation foundations, and industrial-corporate foundations. Public grants have also been an important source of funds, especially for scientific research and on-the-ground conservation projects. Conservation easements in the Malpai Borderlands are relatively inexpensive by national standards—generally around $100 per acre—but the size of the parcels involved means that large amounts of money are required: Protecting a 10,000-acre ranch is a million-dollar proposition, and there are about 150,000 acres of private land in the area that are still vulnerable to subdivision.

ECOLOGICAL CONSEQUENCES OF SUBDIVISION

What are the Malpai Group and its supporters achieving by preventing subdivision? The beauty of unfragmented, wide-open spaces is a signature of the West, and the Borderlands are no exception—but I leave it to photographs to convey this. For Drum Hadley, the preeminent goal is preserving the cultural practices and knowledges of Southwestern ranching—"products of metaphors unavailable in other places," as he puts it—and this cannot be done without large, open landscapes. For most people, however, the relevant measures of Malpai's activities are ecological ones: species, communities, biodiversity, watersheds. These are complicated things to study by themselves, let alone in relation to subdivision and development. Compared to livestock grazing and even to fire, subdivision has received little systematic attention from ecologists. Although a number of studies have examined wildlife and vegetation along urban-to-rural gradients, very few have focused on "exurban" development—that is, the building of houses in remote sites dominated by native vegetation. The ecological consequences of the recent rush to retire, vacation, or telecommute in such locations are therefore poorly understood.

State Route 80 passing through the Krentz family's ranch, which is protected by a Malpai Group conservation easement.

Preliminary evidence clearly shows that rural residential development is much further advanced than previously recognized. Since 1950, the area of land in the coterminous U.S. occupied at densities of ten to forty acres per home has increased five-fold, to nearly one-quarter of the country's land base. The number of people in an average household is declining, even as the average physical size of houses and residential lots is increasing. Although much of this expansion has taken place as "suburban sprawl" around major cities, low-density development is also growing rapidly in more remote locations, especially where various environmental "amenities" can be found: near national parks and forests; along coastlines, rivers, and lakes; and in areas endowed with attractive scenery, climate, recreational opportunities, and wildlife. The most famous such locales—Aspen, Sun Valley, Jackson Hole—are associated with great wealth, and "McMansions" and "starter castles" can be found all over the New West. But the phenomenon is hardly restricted to the upper classes: There are countless ten- to forty-acre lots with trailers and doublewides as well, and more than 60 percent of counties in the Rocky Mountain states experienced more rapid rural than urban population growth from 1990 to 1998. It appears Americans are staging yet another "back to the land" movement, this time stripped of any idealistic pretensions to self-sufficiency, Jeffersonian agrarianism, or democratic collectivism. The goal instead seems to be individual immersion in "nature," whether for retirement and leisure or vigorous recreation, assisted by all manner of technology, infrastructure, and services.

Studies from metropolitan areas suggest that the ecological ramifications of subdivision are significant. Increasing housing density has been shown to correlate with declining native species richness of plants, insects, amphibians, pollinator bees, birds, and rodents. Overall diversity may increase at intermediate densities, as people import plants for landscaping, which attract different insects and wildlife. But native species tend to decline in abundance while more common, human-adapted species increase. Lower-density development entails more roads per housing unit, which fragments habitat and creates corridors for the movement of invasive plants and animals. After houses are first built, many native species may persist for years or even decades before the alterations to their habitats trigger noticeable changes in their populations.

Studies of more remote, rural residential development are wholly lacking from the Southwest, but research in the Rocky Mountain region indicates that the effects on ecosystems and biological diversity are serious and multifaceted, even at low housing densities. A study in Colorado compared the plants, songbirds, and carnivores on ranches, ungrazed protected areas, and ranchettes. It found that non-native plants and animals were more common on ranchettes, due not only to landscaping and pets but also to invasive responses among wildlife species. Common bird species such as magpies and robins were attracted to the habitats created around houses, while house cats and dogs ventured out into undeveloped areas, driving away native wildlife. These effects were most pronounced within one hundred meters of roads and houses, but some could be detected at more than three times that distance. Notably, the study found that non-native plants were significantly less common on ranches than on ungrazed protected areas or ranchettes.

The great battles over the Western Range have focused on the federal lands, especially Forest Service and BLM lands, if only because that is where the public has legal standing to press its views. But scientists are increasingly convinced that the private lands are more important, ecologically speaking: They tend to be located at sites with more water and more productive soils, which are generally found at lower elevations, with warmer temperatures and longer growing seasons. These sites attract animals of all kinds, including humans. A series of studies in the Greater Yellowstone Ecosystem, including Yellowstone National Park and surrounding counties, found that rural homes overlapped significantly with prime bird habitats, and that less than half of the best habitat type was more than one kilometer from a house—even though more than 70 percent of the overall area is public land. For some wildlife species that migrate between high and low elevations seasonally, it appears that Yellowstone National Park may be a population sink—a place where mortality outpaces reproduction—fed each year by population source areas on nearby, privately owned valley bottoms. The same pattern probably obtains elsewhere: 90 percent of threatened and endangered species inhabit private lands, and two-thirds of them rely on private lands for the majority of their habitat. Nature reserves account for only about 5 percent of the nation's land base, according to a recent assessment, and they are predominantly located at higher elevations and on the least productive soils. If biological diversity conservation is to be

Mexican gold poppies on the Krentzes' ranch in spring.

A rock structure for erosion control on the Malpai Ranch.

achieved, it is clear that private lands will be crucially important, and it is precisely the private lands that are most likely to be developed.

———

The Malpai Group has not sponsored scientific research on the effects of subdivision in the Rodeo-Portal area, and by now it is probably too late: the changes are already in motion and no baseline data exist for comparison. The ecological values of the Borderlands can be documented, studied, and treasured, but how much they would be degraded by development cannot be known in detail until and unless development happens. One can think about it hypothetically, though. Sixteen forty-acre homesites can be put on a square mile of land. On the best range in the Borderlands, the same area will support about sixteen cattle. Which has a greater ecological footprint, one cow or one house?

CHAPTER 7

AGAINST LONG ODDS

The Malpai Borderlands Group has been widely acclaimed as a model for "community-based conservation." Something must account for Malpai's accomplishments, and in theory that something ought to be identifiable and transferable. But what *is* that something? The history presented in the preceding chapters does suggest a handful of lessons or principles that may have broader application. However, it also demonstrates that the Malpai Group has benefited from a number of chance events and exceptional circumstances, without which the effort might well have foundered. It would be premature to declare Malpai an unqualified success, moreover, since its mission is still far from realized and may yet prove impossible. The Malpai Group is working against longstanding trends and institutions in the administration and politics of public lands, in the economy, and in the ecological patterns and processes of the landscape itself. To learn from it in any truly constructive way, one must acknowledge

its weaknesses as well as its strengths. What are the factors that have made its accomplishments possible? In what ways has it not yet succeeded, and how might it ultimately fail? These are the questions that must be answered to assess Malpai's implications for conservation elsewhere, and in particular for the possibility of a New Western Range.

FORTUNE AND WORK

A great deal of the Malpai Group's success seems attributable to good fortune: the fact that the Gray Ranch drew The Nature Conservancy into the area just when it did; the presence of Drum Hadley, with his unique combination of local and extra-local relationships, cultural and environmental values, and family resources; the coincidence of the Malpai Agenda with emerging federal interest in ecosystem management; and the proximity of Jim Brown and Ray Turner, whose stature among ecologists lent Malpai's efforts a scientific credibility that might otherwise have been difficult to establish. It was also a stroke of luck that the Conservancy had stumbled in its early handling of the Gray, causing John Sawhill to take it "off line." This meant that the Malpai Group was able to work directly with the Conservancy's national office, with all its capabilities and contacts, instead of through the New Mexico or Arizona chapters, where intrastate environmental politics might have bogged it down. Finally, an extraordinary sequence of positive stories gave the Malpai Group a recurrent presence in national media: the announcement of the sale of the Gray Ranch to the Animas Foundation (1993), the Magoffins' efforts to save the population of leopard frogs on their ranch (1994), the Grassbank (1995–98), Warner Glenn's jaguar encounter (1996), and

Bill McDonald's MacArthur award (1998). Stories such as these seem to have had a snowball effect, attracting local and regional reporters, profiles in magazines, follow-up stories, and heightened interest generally among politicians, bureaucrats, and foundations. Even after a decade in operation, the Malpai Group still stands out against conventional expectations.

Behind this good fortune, however, lies an exceptional amount of work. The Gray Ranch sale couldn't have happened without two years of effort by the Hadleys and the Conservancy; the Magoffins had to haul all that water; the jaguar didn't just present itself to Warner; and so forth. The individuals described in previous chapters only begin to convey the full scope of the Malpai Group's work. Ben Brown became program

director for the Animas Foundation, coordinating scientific research, fire and wildlife management, and community outreach; he now works as science coordinator for the Malpai Group. Kelly Cash, a communications staff person with the Conservancy in California, has helped manage national media relations for Malpai since its founding. Bill Miller, Jr., a lifelong rancher in the Peloncillo Mountains, served as president of the board for many years and has given countless talks and presentations on the Malpai Group's behalf. He also has worked closely with ranchers to craft their conservation easements, helping build confidence and tailor terms to match each landowner's specific needs and concerns. Reese Woodling, a former Peloncillos rancher and current Malpai president, chaired a subcommittee that

Bill Miller working in the gun shop he opened in Rodeo upon his retirement.

MONITORING

How to detect and interpret ecological change in the Borderlands is a far more complex issue than one might think. What should be measured? Where? How frequently? And given the extreme variability of rainfall and plant growth—which ramifies through other components of the ecosystem in complex ways—how do we distinguish between changes that happen "naturally" and those due to human management decisions? Even monitoring strategies that seem simple, such as measuring vegetation once a year at fixed locations, turn out to be both labor-intensive (and therefore expensive to maintain, especially in the long term) and fraught with scientific and methodological challenges. It is not surprising that public agencies have struggled to implement and sustain effective monitoring programs for their lands.

The Malpai Borderlands Group has made a major, ongoing commitment to monitoring in their planning area. Malpai's program builds on the one instituted by the Animas Foundation and The Nature Conservancy on the Gray Ranch, where a network of more than one hundred monitoring sites was established pursuant to their conservation easement. Each site is "read" at least once every five years, using a method that involves identifying and counting every plant along a series of hundred-meter lines. In this way the composition of the vegetation (the presence and relative abundance of different species) and the density (how much of the ground is covered by the base or canopy of plants) can be estimated for representative areas of the ranch. From such information, inferences can be made about the structure and function of ecosystems over time.

What and how to monitor depends on the ecosystem in question, the management goals and practices there, and the degree of precision needed to make the results useful. One of the earliest tasks of the Malpai Group was to develop a monitoring protocol that would meet the needs and expectations of all the stakeholders in the area: two state land departments, two state game and fish departments, four federal agencies, and the ranchers themselves. Based on input from the agencies and from outside scientists, a "point-intercept" method was chosen, similar to the one from the Gray Ranch but with sites read every three years instead of five. Sites were initially installed on a project-by-project basis: on each of the four grassbank ranches and in conjunction with each prescribed fire. All ranchers that enter into conservation easements with Malpai are offered this monitoring program as well, and to date all have agreed to participate. There are currently more than two hundred monitoring sites in the planning area.

Monitoring is not research: It can detect changes but it cannot by itself identify the causes behind them. Monitoring data from burned and unburned sites, for example, has documented increases in perennial grasses and declines in woody species following fires, but the data also suggest that other factors—such as the timing and amount of rainfall—may strongly determine the effects of burning on vegetation. To make the monitoring program more illuminating, the Malpai Group has recently decided to integrate it more closely with ongoing research efforts into the causes and dynamics of vegetation change. This will involve selecting sites more systematically to capture the range of ecological conditions in the Borderlands and to target areas where change is most likely or most amenable to management action: for example, in transition zones between grassland and shrubland. Grazing exclosures are likely to be added to detect changes associated with livestock, and a greater effort will be mounted to monitor rainfall, soil moisture, and temperature. This more selective sample of sites will be monitored every year, in hopes of obtaining data with a finer resolution.

spent three years investigating alternative marketing strategies for ranchers in the area; he also edits a newsletter that Malpai produces for local ranchers. Pete Sundt has worked for ten years monitoring vegetation in connection with fires, grassbanking, easements, and experiments. Wendy Glenn and Mary McDonald have managed the office and the finances, respectively, assisted in recent years by Carrie Krentz, another rancher in the area. From the Conservancy's Tucson office, Peter Warren has served as full-time Malpai coordinator since 1995, writing proposals and heading up relations with state and federal agencies regarding fire, endangered species, and other regulatory issues. The list of other contributors—scientists, agency personnel, foundation officials, and volunteers—is too long to review here.

Coordinating all this work has entailed weekly conference calls (which occur at six or seven in the morning, the only time everyone can be near a phone) and scores of meetings each year. The calls are expensive, but there is no other way to keep so many people, who are so spread out, up to date on one another's activities. The meetings serve both to conduct business and to keep other partners up to date as well: The Malpai Group hosts a science conference every year or two, a get-together for the local community every year, and a dedicated meeting of agency representatives annually. About once a year they hold a three-day workshop for groups who want a more in-depth look at what they are doing, and another newsletter is produced for the broader community of Malpai supporters. Capitalizing on the opportunities presented by fate, in short, has required significant and well-managed effort.

In one sense the Malpai Group's mission is a conservative one: to maintain the current land use and culture of the area. This cannot be achieved simply by preventing change, however, because the Western Range is like a leaking lifeboat: It must be repaired or rebuilt if it is to persist. Congress seems unable to replace it with something new, yet it cannot be abandoned altogether because it is what ties private, state, and federal lands together. The Malpai Group's work reflects this predicament: The inherent difficulty of changing the status quo is compounded by the necessity of working within a system of institutions and policies inherited from another era. The most time-consuming challenges have been regulatory and inter-agency ones. At the meeting on the Gray Ranch in April 1993, it was recognized that a comprehensive fire plan was needed: a template that would

Reese Woodling placed a conservation easement on his ranch in the Peloncillo Mountains.

guide and permit prescribed fires across landownership types in the area. Twelve years later, in 2005, such a plan is only nearly complete, and the delay was due largely to the intricacies of inter- and intra-agency politics, policies, and procedures, such as those described in Chapter 5 regarding the ridgenose rattlesnake. Support is needed not only from each agency, but also from numerous individuals within each agency. Every time a relevant agency position turns over—which has happened with virtually all of them since 1994, from field staff to regional, state, and national directors—the Malpai Group has had to invest time familiarizing the newcomer with what appears, relative to their prior experience, to be a novel and unconventional situation.

In addition to formal issues, moreover, there are habits and assumptions that must be suspended or changed, one individual at a time. In 2002, for example, the Malpai Group initiated meetings with state and federal agencies to craft a Habitat Conservation Plan, a legal agreement designed to ensure Endangered Species Act compliance for the activities of the Malpai Group and participating ranchers on non-federal lands in the area. (By statute, a Habitat Conservation Plan cannot apply to federal lands.) Like the comprehensive fire plan, this was an effort to achieve a regulatory economy of scale—an umbrella agreement to replace the conventional and more time-consuming case-by-case approach. Participants discussed every species that is or might be listed in the area, including those that are rare in either state—forty-six species in all—and every activity that might impact them, including fire, grazing, ranch management, and various kinds of vegetation manipulation. At the outset, it was clear that several agency biologists considered all or most of these activities potential threats to rare species and thus expected that they would need to be covered by the plan. It was simply a given, for them, that every aspect of ranching is inherently detrimental to native plants and animals.

Phil, Ben, and Rob Krentz on their ranch. Their ancestors started the ranch nearly a century ago; they sold a conservation easement to the Malpai Group.

A Habitat Conservation Plan extends protection from Endangered Species Act liability, however, only in exchange for assuming an ongoing burden of proof. If the plan covered grazing, for example, the Malpai Group would have to demonstrate that grazing was not resulting in take above approved levels. Without coverage, by contrast, the Fish and Wildlife Service would bear the burden of demonstrating that take had occurred. It required half a dozen three-hour meetings to arrive at agreement that in almost every case, neither party could meet such a burden. The ecological interactions were too complex and indirect to permit demonstration either way. One could imagine scenarios that might result in take, but only one seemed sufficiently plausible to justify coverage under a plan: prescribed fires in the watershed above the San Bernardino National Wildlife Refuge, where heavy sedimentation might impact protected fish if torrential rains occurred before recovery of herbaceous vegetation.

Even with good fortune, then, the Malpai Group has required an extraordinary measure of patience and persistence. It could easily have dissipated out of frustration or simple fatigue, or its own successes could have opened internal rifts over who received how much credit. Instead, the people involved have mustered a sense of dedication and enthusiasm that is collectively self-reinforcing: What looks impossible is tackled, and each achievement breeds further confidence and determination. Bill McDonald credits this dynamic to the early discussion group and in particular to Jim Corbett's influence. In 1991–92, he corresponded at length with Jim, whose letters always required a dictionary and multiple readings. "Jim really took the black and white out of issues," he recalls, "and made you see the gray. He made you look inside yourself." The discussions not only yielded a consensus agenda for action, then, but also a collective sense that what Malpai is about is "bigger than any of us," and an inner confidence to attempt things they never would have considered feasible before. Bill says that this combination of shared humility and audacious conviction has enabled the Group to persevere when it might have come apart.

COMMUNITY

That the Malpai Group is an example of "community-based conservation" is easy to see and even easier to say, but it is quite difficult to specify what "community" means or to whom exactly it refers. The term is used much more frequently by people talking about the Malpai Group than it is by the members themselves. For outsiders, it generally means that conservation occurs with the active participation and support of local residents, rather than being imposed on them by outside powers or experts. Like ecosystem management and "Last Great Places," community-based conservation seeks to integrate human economic activities into biological and ecological conservation, on the premise that resource-based livelihoods will benefit from good stewardship (and ultimately all livelihoods are resource-based). All of this fits the Malpai case well enough. But applying the label "community-based" does nothing to explain how such a harmonious integration of people and environment is actually achieved.

Malpai's mission statement pledges to protect a "community of human, plant and animal life in our borderlands region," but the first word of the following sentence—"together"—more accurately captures the spirit of the Malpai Group's approach. Its bylaws do not require consensus decision-making, but as far as I know every vote of the board has been unanimous. Meanwhile, the relationships Malpai has developed have produced multiple communities that overlap and intersect with each other: donors and foundations, agency employees, scientists, hunters, private sector conservationists from the U.S. and overseas, even writers and artists. The local community of ranchers was already there, of course, and in some sense it forms the core around which the others have coalesced. Private landowners dominate the board and thus hold formal power, but their dependence on outside partners and institutions is obvious. Without the larger communities' help, the core community cannot withstand the pressures of subdivision and development on private land and of competing political claims on public lands. Holding this complex of relationships together, then, is not so much a matter of locals versus outsiders, or private interests versus public ones, but rather of mutual interdependence: a sense that shared goals can only be achieved cooperatively. This, in turn, requires mutual respect at the level of everyday interactions. In Bill McDonald's words, "You begin to have less interest in labels and more interest in individuals."

Even the lessons that can be drawn from the Malpai Group, then, undermine the notion of using it as a model. Patience, trust, communication, consensus, and an emphasis on social and ecological processes rather than predetermined or fixed outcomes—these may be taken as instructive or exemplary characteristics of how the Malpai Group works. As John Cook insists, however, Malpai has succeeded precisely because it has not sought to impose a "model" from someplace else, but instead has remained flexible and adaptive to its own particular circumstances and values. "It's all about a human ethic," he says, which must come about voluntarily. Distilling a model for use elsewhere thus may violate the very thing it purports to capture.

PITFALLS

Notwithstanding all its achievements, the Malpai Group remains a long way from making its mission statement a reality. Three kinds of potential pitfalls stand out: economic, political, and ecological. They are interrelated, and they point to the ways in which Malpai is dependent on larger-scale processes over which it has little or no control.

Ranching is probably the most ecologically sustainable portion of the U.S. beef industry, but it is increasingly marginal economically. Grazing native plants to grow and reproduce is exactly how cattle evolved (along with many of the plants they eat), and unlike modern crop agriculture or feedlot animal production, range livestock production does not require large inputs of fossil fuels, chemicals, or other outside resources. At every other step of the process from ranch to dinner table, however, industrial-style innovations have enabled economies of scale and market consolidations that have steadily eroded the share of the consumers' food dollar that ranchers receive. Millions of consumers and thousands of ranchers are linked by a mere handful of firms that dominate the feeding and packing sectors, such that market prices for cattle are wholly beyond ranchers' control. Costs of production have steadily increased over the past thirty years, especially for land, while cattle prices have stagnated.

Alternative marketing is widely touted as a potential way out of this problem, and the Malpai Group has investigated it in detail. Numerous organic, natural, grass-finished, or wildlife-friendly beef enterprises have been launched in recent years, and in a few places they have been successful. But far more have failed than have succeeded. A processing plant is needed, with USDA-certified inspectors. The costs of such a facility require a steady and significant volume of animals. Even if the Malpai Group could find a processor to work with (which is unlikely at present), the ranches in the area cannot produce a year-round supply due to the seasonality of precipitation (grass-finished beef needs to come from cattle that have eaten green grass in the final month of their lives) and the logistics of rounding up animals on the range. There are numerous other hurdles to clear, and various other possible strategies that could be pursued. Suffice to say that Malpai's Beef Marketing Committee reached the conclusion that the upfront costs could not be justified in view of the risks involved.

In short, the goal of sustaining ranching as the primary livelihood in the Malpai area may ultimately prove unattainable. Most of the ranchers already have other income sources, anyway: the Glenns guide hunters, Edward Elbrock operates heavy equipment, and Rich Winkler is an attorney. Several others work for the Malpai Group, and a few have pensions or outside wealth to draw on. The point is that livestock production is already a marginal proposition, especially when the rains fail. Ultimately, its competitive advantage is equivalent to its ecological sustainability: The grasses and cattle can grow on their own, with minimal human inputs. More industrial forms of beef production may nonetheless someday achieve lower per-unit costs—at the expense of ecosystems elsewhere—and make ranching economically obsolete.

Grazing leases can be canceled if the lessee does not run cattle for an extended period of time, so the economic pressures quickly spill over into political ones. And the political processes that will determine the fate of state and federal lands in the Malpai area run through Phoenix, Santa Fe, Washington, D.C., and the Ninth Circuit Court of Appeals in San Francisco. By filing lawsuits that seize on federal agencies' chronic inability to meet the procedural requirements of the Endangered Species Act and the National Environmental Policy Act, groups such as the Center for Biological Diversity have pursued their goal of eliminating public lands grazing, even if it means eliminating ranching and ranchers altogether. These groups steadfastly hold to the Clementsian

assumption of the Western Range: that ecological restoration will happen by itself if livestock are removed from the range. Accordingly, their strategy is entirely negative: prevent the agencies from actively doing anything—renewing a grazing permit, for example—either by court order or by inducing them into passivity. Inaction is no guarantee that an imperiled species will persist, as we saw in Chapter 5, but without an action there is no liability under the law. Given the scientific uncertainty surrounding many endangered species, moreover, the potential for bureaucratic gridlock is high. The efforts of the Malpai Group and its agency partners to overcome these problems have been extraordinary and generally successful, but it is entirely conceivable that grazing leases could be lost "independent of any action taken by the parties" involved, thereby unraveling Malpai's conservation easements and fragmenting the landscape.

One way to counter both the economic and political pressures against continued ranching in the Malpai Borderlands is to succeed in restoring a significant portion of the grassland areas lost to shrub dominance in the past 115 years. Here, however, ecological pitfalls emerge. Exactly where and how to restore grasses, how quickly it can be accomplished, and how much more grass can be

Animas Mountains, Gray Ranch.

expected are questions without precise answers at this time. It may entail significant changes in established management practices: moving livestock more frequently or over larger areas; destocking more rapidly and deeply during drought; using goats to overbrowse undesirable shrubs; or amalgamating herds from neighboring ranches. For periods of time, it may entail destocking altogether. If it could be done, though, it would both augment the productive capacity of ranch operations and satisfy all but the most extreme critics of grazing.

Even with the best possible effort, however, it is likely that restoring grasslands will take decades or longer to achieve. Historic erosion of topsoil may be irremediable in the shorter term, limiting the potential for perennial grass production no matter how the range is managed. Returning fire to the entire landscape—itself a long-term proposition—should gradually tilt the competitive balance toward grasses. But when, where and how to burn are still subjects for research, and although fire is necessary, it will not be sufficient by itself to reverse shrub encroachment. It is also uncertain whether a pre-settlement fire regime (in which most sites burn once every eight to twelve years on average) would be compatible with commercial livestock production as currently practiced. Many ranches, especially smaller ones, cannot afford to rest large areas for the periods of time necessary to build up fine fuels and allow recovery after a fire. Finally, the evidence from McKinney Flats and other research sites indicates that climate—especially the timing and amount of rainfall—will determine vegetation much more strongly than grazing, fire, or other management actions.

A NEW WESTERN RANGE

If the obstacles to success appear daunting, it's because they are—but pessimistic despair is no alternative. The Malpai Borderlands Group has succeeded in forestalling development and in refocusing the debate about ranching and conservation away from cattle, at least within the planning area. Whereas ranchers elsewhere are constantly on the defensive due to the presumption that cattle are not only destructive but are also *the* issue to be resolved, Malpai has turned attention toward the specter of subdivision, the challenge of fire, the complexity of ecosystems, and the pragmatic details of conserving species such as the Chiricahua leopard frog. This has created a buffer of sorts, a space where the ordinary presumption against innovation is at least suspended, if not reversed. Within this space, the outlines of a New Western Range can be discerned.

It begins with an emphasis on private lands. Even if they are a minority of the overall landscape, they are likely to be of greater ecological consequence than the surrounding state and federal holdings. They are also the lands most vulnerable to subdivision and development. Although ranches may be dependent on public grazing leases for their economic viability, the public lands are ecologically dependent on the continued well-being of the adjacent private ranch lands. The Achilles' heel of the Western Range was its assumption that the highest economic use of private lands would always be livestock grazing. This is no longer the case, but it can be remedied. Unilaterally stripping those lands of development potential—by zoning, for example—cannot but provoke a counterproductive backlash among ranch owners. There is strong evidence that most ranchers do not want to see their lands subdivided and developed, however, and voluntary approaches can build on this commitment. Keeping large landscapes open and unfragmented is in the public interest, for ecological and fiscal reasons as well as aesthetic ones. Conservation easements allow ranch owners to realize the equity value of their lands' development potential without sacrificing this public good.

As the Malpai experience demonstrates, conservation easements on private land must be linked to grazing leases on public lands, and the logical next step is to acknowledge this interdependency and reciprocate. If a private ranch has renounced the option of development, the associated grazing leases should be extended accordingly. This could be done permanently (using ninety-nine-year leases, for example) or for periods of, say, twenty-five years (in which case the development rights would essentially be leased by a conservation organization). Requirements for responsible management of leased lands would remain in place. This would restore the broken premise of the Western Range that a ranch's value rests on its productive capacity, such that ranchers' private incentives align with the public's interest in healthy rangelands.

A second flaw in the Western Range was its Clementsian assumptions about plant ecology: that livestock grazing is the key variable in vegetation dynamics, and that livestock removal will reverse changes caused by past grazing. There are instances where these assumptions hold, but there are many others where they do not. In drier settings such as the Southwest, livestock exclusion is neither necessary nor sufficient to achieve most conservation goals. To focus on livestock alone, to the exclusion of climate, fire, erosion, invasive species, urbanization, and other factors, is both politically crippling and ecologically naïve. The Malpai case demonstrates that confronting ecological complexity with collaborative adaptive management and scientific research can be both socially and ecologically constructive.

Third, the Western Range also failed to recognize the variability of rangeland ecosystems across space and time. There is far too much diversity in the rangelands of the West for a single administrative paradigm to accommodate. Likewise, any given range is far too variable for a static management prescription such as is currently imposed under the concept of carrying capacity. In the most influential paper of the past half-century of range science, Mark Westoby, Brian Walker, and Imanuel Noy-Meir summarize the regulatory implications of state and transition models this way:

Drop the assumption that inaction or conservative grazing is safe. In many situations moderate grazing leads to range deterioration. Sometimes very heavy grazing is a constructive thing to do. Often, burning is a constructive thing to do. Legislation and regulations need to free managers to intervene positively. Where possible, regulation should focus not on stocking rates but on changes in the actual state of the land or the vegetation.

What is required, in short, is greater flexibility on the part of both government agencies and ranchers. Stocking rates should be allowed to vary with forage production, to levels both higher and lower than existing norms. Management actions such as burning, rest, seeding, shrub removal, or intensive grazing should be used opportunistically, when the right climatic conditions present themselves. This means that agencies must be able to authorize such actions very quickly or on a contingency basis, rather than on a pre-determined or business-as-usual timetable. The overarching goal is management that matches the ecological variability of the underlying resource. Whether this can be achieved within the existing framework of federal land ownership and administration is unclear: Some degree of decentralization or devolution may be unavoidable.

Finally, a New Western Range must emphasize social, ecological, and economic diversity. The Malpai Group has succeeded not by focusing on the local community but by expanding outward to other communities, incorporating the views and values of environmentalists, scientists, and other non-ranchers. It has embraced "the health and unreduced diversity of the native biotic community," rather than simply forage or livestock, as the fundamental basis for, and goal of, effective management. Through grants, partnerships, easements, and a handful of products such as Warner Glenn's jaguar book, Malpai has also begun to diversify the revenue sources that contribute to preserving ranching on their landscape. Cattle alone are already insufficient as the sole basis for most ranches, and a great deal more needs to be done to remunerate good land managers for the public values they produce: improved wildlife habitat, enhanced watersheds and flood control, open space protection, and so on.

The Western Range is broken and much maligned, but it has one singular achievement to its credit: It held vast landscapes of mixed private, state, and federal ownership together in large, unfragmented units. The New West is rapidly eroding this legacy through economic, political, and legal challenges, pushing the private lands into the hands of developers and exurbanites and the public lands into the sway of environmentalists and recreation enthusiasts. If the public lands and a few additional "protected" areas were sufficient to sustain the ecological values of the West's rangelands, such an arrangement might not seem so shortsighted. But they are not sufficient, and once the process of fragmentation has begun it is generally impossible to reverse. There is no single model that can be abstracted from the Malpai Borderlands Group and applied, top-down, in other locations, because such an imposition is intrinsically inconsistent with the principle of a land ethic. There are countless, unheralded grassroots groups scattered across the West, however, whose goals are similar to those of the Malpai Group and whose efforts could be facilitated by a New Western Range.

Water storage and distribution systems, such as this one on the Krentz ranch, play critical roles in managing Southwestern cattle operations.

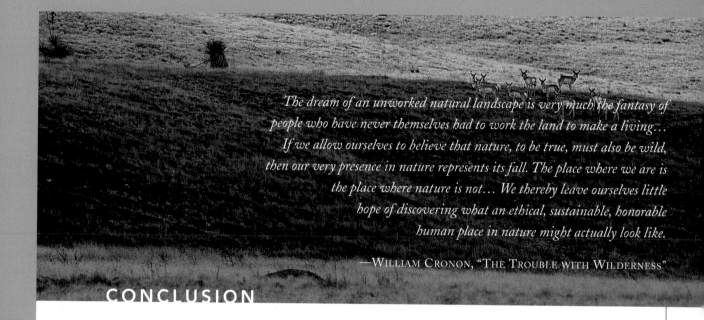

The dream of an unworked natural landscape is very much the fantasy of people who have never themselves had to work the land to make a living... If we allow ourselves to believe that nature, to be true, must also be wild, then our very presence in nature represents its fall. The place where we are is the place where nature is not... We thereby leave ourselves little hope of discovering what an ethical, sustainable, honorable human place in nature might actually look like.

—William Cronon, "The Trouble with Wilderness"

CONCLUSION

WORKING WILDERNESS

For now, only the cow can make the wildlands of the arid West a motherland for human communities.

—Jim Corbett,
Sanctuary for All Life

On July 2, 1991, Dale Cureton drove to the southeast corner of the Rocker M Ranch to repair a windmill. As he worked he noticed that the wind was not blowing from the southwest that day, as it usually did, but from the east, gusting to thirty or forty miles per hour. Immediately downwind from the windmill was an area that his employer had paid more than $60,000 to treat with chemicals eight years before, when Dale had just started working as the manager there. The chemicals had killed the creosote bushes, as intended, and the ground was now covered with annual three-awn grasses. But amidst the pale brown stems Dale could see new creosote bush seedlings becoming established. In a few more years, they would over-

top the grasses, spread their roots out, and once again dominate the site.

In their parched condition, the three-awns were poor forage for cattle, but they were perfect fuel to burn out the seedling creosote bushes. On a typical day, with winds from the southwest, a fire there might move east onto the Glenns' Malpai Ranch. But with the strong east wind that day, Dale judged that the benefits of burning far outweighed the risks. He lit the grass on fire, sat down, and watched the flames move away to the west. A while later, Warner and his daughter, Kelly Glenn, drove up. "You think we oughta try to put it out?" Warner asked Dale. "No, I think it's doing just fine," Dale answered. "I do too," Warner replied, "I just don't want anybody to get in trouble."

Dale Cureton very nearly did get in trouble that day. The Forest Service helicopter sat idly on the road, unable to find a nearby body of water large enough to fill its bucket. The hand crews raced around trying to scrape fire lines through the grass, but the wind blew the flames right across their work and underneath their trucks. The fire burned itself out when it reached the edge of the area that had been treated in 1983, just as Dale had expected. Nonetheless, the Forest Service threatened to fine him $600 per hour for suppression costs, and they probably would have if they had had any proof that he'd started the blaze on purpose. He left the Rocker M in 2000, and he never participated in the Malpai Borderlands Group. "I don't have time to go to all those meetings," he explains.

That the Geronimo Trail fire was started on purpose, to achieve a management objective, has until now been a quietly shared secret in the Borderlands. Only Dale Cureton's permission and the statute of limitations allow me to reveal it here, and I do so neither to celebrate an illegal act nor to suggest that the Malpai Group condones it—they do not, and all of their fire work has been premised on the need to work within the law. Rather, I wish to consider the questions the fire poses, which in many ways are the central questions of the Malpai story as a whole: Whom should we trust with the authority to manage Western rangelands? Whom *do* we trust, and why? What role should people play in these vast, relatively undeveloped, and fantastically diverse landscapes?

The laws and policies that sent the Forest Service to put out the fire that day are state and federal ones, intended to apply everywhere and all the time, motivated by the general threats that wildfires can pose to people and property. They are indifferent to the ecological role of fire in Southwestern landscapes and to the factors that Dale Cureton considered decisive in choosing to do what he did: the history and ecology of that particular site, on that particular day, when the threats to people and property were negligible. His objective was to prevent a transition to a less desirable state of vegetation; it was a textbook instance of "opportunistic management for rangelands not at equilibrium." Securing a permit to set the fire would have taken months, possibly years, by which time the opportunity to achieve the objective would have passed. The public has every right to oversee the use of its lands, but to what extent are the ecological circumstances of Western rangelands comparable to the situation Dale faced that day?

The natural history of the Southwest has been singled out for sustained study for over a century, by many of the nation's most eminent scientists and research institutions. Leading figures in botany, ecology, wildlife, and geology—people such as Forrest Shreve, Frederic Clements, Aldo Leopold, and Kirk Bryan—cut their professional teeth in the Southwest. Yet it remains a region whose landscapes challenge scientific understanding and defy attempts at control or prediction. The Western Range was designed largely to restore and conserve perennial grasses, for example. Yet an estimated 84 percent of Southwestern grasslands—more than 8.5 million acres—have seen a significant shift toward woody plant species, and more than 5 million acres have become so dominated by brush that they can no longer carry a fire. Without fire, restoring grasses is probably impossible.

The practices that produced this unintended consequence—fire suppression and year-round livestock grazing at static carrying capacities—are examples of what ecologists C. S. Holling and Gary Meffe have termed the "command and control approach" to natural resource management. Valuable resources—timber and grass, in this case—are managed in isolation from their ecosystems in an effort to produce large and reliable yields. Success in the short term blinds managers to the fact that their efforts are simplifying ecosystems and making them less resilient to natural variability and disturbances such as drought or fire. The resulting "pathology of natural resource management" is a vicious cycle in which ecological breakdowns provoke still more strenuous efforts at command and control, further compromising ecosystem resilience and leading to further breakdowns. The histories of forest and range management in the Southwest both conform to this pattern, as does the Forest Service's response to the Geronimo Trail Road fire. What the Malpai Group has been working towards ever since that day is to overcome this pathology. Their emphasis on ecological processes and the whole biotic community leads to management practices that strive, in Holling and Meffe's words, "to retain critical types and ranges of natural variation in ecosystems."

The Malpai Borderlands is not technically a wilderness, but it is indisputably wild: 1,250 square miles of land with scarcely a paved road and fewer than one hundred inhabitants. Less than 1 percent of it has ever been plowed, and only a small portion of that remains in crop production today. If one chooses to equate wild with dangerous, the Borderlands offers a portfolio of perils.

A person lost, naïve, or poorly prepared might perish from thirst, frost, heat stroke, or rattlesnake bite. The Borderlands fulfills the aesthetic notion of wild as well. At almost any spot on any day, natural beauty will strike from some direction or at some moment. Newcomers are most susceptible to the big beauty—sunsets or mountain vistas or monsoon thunderheads—but it comes in all sizes and scales. With greater familiarity, one eventually sees it everywhere. It is a land that has not been domesticated, where natural processes and native organisms predominate.

None of this changes the fact that the Borderlands has also been altered by humans and that much of this alteration has been for the worse. Grizzly bears, beavers, and wolves have been missing for decades. Overgrazing and drought have reduced perennial grasses, sometimes nearly to nil, and intentional fire suppression has helped shrubby plants to take their place across vast areas. Most of the floodplains have been cut by arroyos, rearranging patterns of moisture and therefore vegetation. Non-native and invasive species pose threats to several rare species of fish and frogs. Dirt roads and fences criss-cross the area, and a growing number of recreationists, undocumented immigrants, and Border Patrol vehicles are steadily making their marks: new paths and roads, cut fences, and trash of all sorts.

Understanding the Southwestern range today requires holding these two superficially incompatible ideas in one's head simultaneously: wildness and sublime natural beauty on the one hand, persistent human use and ecological change on the other. Recognizing that humans are part of nature (rather than opposed to and outside of it) and that Native Americans also altered the landscape long before Europeans arrived, are only pre-liminary and rather abstract steps. Acknowledging the role ranching has played in degrading the land, directly and indirectly, still does not address the relevant question: What is to be done now?

For most of the twentieth century, scientists and conservationists alike believed that ecological damage would heal itself if people were excluded and past dis-turbances such as livestock grazing were removed. It was largely on this premise that national parks and wilder-nesses were created, and it continues to inform a naïve belief in some quarters that Southwestern rangelands can be restored simply by removing livestock. Take away that premise, however, and the wilderness model looks rather weak. The idea of landscapes untouched by humans has been discredited: Native Americans affected these lands, particularly by the use of fire; Euro-Americans have likewise affected them by sup-pressing fire. However beautiful and ecologically signifi-cant wilderness areas may be, they are not sufficient by themselves to sustain biological diversity—for that mat-ter, all the public lands in the West taken together are not sufficient. Some way of integrating conservation and human use must be found, and rangelands are the most promising site for it. More than 400 million acres in size, roughly half private land and half public, they have been used and sometimes abused, but they are closer to a natural state than any other lands that have seen so much human occupation and activity. Jim Cor-bett was right: "In...most of the arid West, ranching is now the only livelihood that is based on human adapta-tion to wild biotic communities."

The meaning of *working wilderness* is two-fold. First, it insists that human work can be compatible with func-tioning wildlands. This is contrary to conventional and legal definitions, which conceive of wilderness as a place where "man is a visitor who does not remain," a land-scape of recreation and contemplation rather than pro-duction and labor. Second, it underscores the point that properly functioning wildlands do work, in the sense that they produce values for humans. Some of these val-ues can be objectified or measured, others are wholly qualitative or subjective. The point is that they do not simply fall from the sky or happen by accident. They are produced by the interaction of natural processes and human activities.

The challenge lies in making these two dimensions of working wilderness complement each other symbiotically: cultivating human activities and livelihoods that work with, rather than against, natural processes. A century ago, capital flooded the West in pursuit of windfall profits from grass and livestock, overwhelming the resilience of the range. For a time, ranchers, agencies, and scientists endeavored to force the range to meet demands and fit models that it could not meet and would not fit: bulldozing mesquites, importing exotic grasses, imposing static carrying capacities. But today, another tsunami of capital has arrived in search of profits from scenic homesites, and ranching has had to renounce its pretensions of control. It can no longer pay for such extravagant investments, and it has learned from experience that they do not work in the long run anyhow. Ranching now presents both a barrier to the current tsunami and a potential path towards a viable land ethic in the arid West. To quote from Jim Corbett's Malpai Agenda again:

Much more is at stake here than the future of a few ranch families. Wildlands teach those for whom they are home an outlook and insights to which others are blind. Some of these lessons take many generations to learn... These lessons come hard, and no society that eradicates or discards those among its members who have acquired this kind of wisdom can mature into a people that is truly at home in its land.

BIBLIOGRAPHIC NOTES

The sources for this book include interviews with past and present Malpai Group members and cooperators; archival records of the Animas Foundation, the Malpai Group, the Coronado National Forest, The Nature Conservancy, the Victorio Company, the U.S. Fish and Wildlife Service, and the Natural Resource Conservation Service; newspaper and magazine articles; government documents; a handful of commercial books and "gray literature" sources; and peer-reviewed academic journals and monographs in a variety of fields. Rather than attempt a comprehensive list, and in order to avoid cluttering the text with citations or footnotes, this essay provides references for all direct quotations and statistics in the preceding chapters and suggests major sources for those readers who seek further information. Unless otherwise noted, details of the history of the Malpai Borderlands Group are drawn from interviews and archival sources.

PREFACE: SUPPRESSING A FIRE, IGNITING A COMMUNITY

The best single source for information on the biological diversity of the Malpai Borderlands is *Biodiversity and Management of the Madrean Archipelago: The Sky Islands of Southwestern United States and Northwestern Mexico* (USDA-Forest Service General Technical Report RM-GTR-264, July 1995; technical coordinators Leonard F. DeBano and five others). It is a proceedings volume based on a conference held in Tucson in September 1994, and it covers the larger "sky island" area of which the Malpai Borderlands are a part. A second, follow-up Madrean Archipelago conference was held in 2004, proceedings of which are expected in August 2005 from the USDA-Forest Service-Rocky Mountain Research Station. For information more specifically focused on the Malpai planning area, see Charles G. Curtin and James H. Brown, "Climate and Herbivory in Structuring the Vegetation of the Malpai Borderlands," pp. 84-94 in *Changing Plant Life of La Frontera*, edited by Grady L. Webster and Conrad J. Bahre (University of New Mexico Press, 2001), and the citations contained therein. A more popular treatment is James H. Brown and

Astrid Kodric-Brown, "Biodiversity on the Borderlands" (*Natural History* April 1996, pp. 58-61).

Only a few scholarly treatments of the Malpai Borderlands Group exist. The most thorough is also the least readily available: Alexander T. Conley, "Learning from the Land, Learning from Each Other: Case Studies of Collaborative Management in Arizona Rangelands" (masters thesis, School of Renewable Natural Resources, University of Arizona, 2003). Less detailed but more widely available discussions include Charles G. Curtin, "Integration of Science and Community-Based Conservation in the Mexico/U.S. Borderlands" (*Conservation Biology* 16(4), August 2002: 880-886) and Mari N. Jensen, "Can Cows and Conservation Mix?" (*BioScience* 51(2), February 2001: 85-90). Two scholars have compared the Malpai Group with other efforts to assert greater local control over land and resources: the Zapatistas in Mexico (Joni Adamson, "Encounter with a Mexican Jaguar: Nature, NAFTA, Militarization, and Ranching in the U.S.-Mexico Borderlands," pp. 221-240 in *Globalization on the Line: Culture, Capital, and Citizenship at U.S. Borders*, edited by Claudia Sadowski-Smith, Palgrave, 2002); and the Kenya Wildlife Service's attempts to collaborate with tribal groups such as the Maasai (Charis M. Thompson, "Ranchers, Scientists, and Grass-roots Development in the United States and Kenya," *Environmental Values* 11(3) (2002): 303-326).

The "gray" literature on the Malpai Group is larger. The best of it is "The Malpai Borderlands Group: Science, Community, and Collaborative Management," prepared by Tom Wolf for the Workshop on Collaborative Resource Management in the Interior West, Red Lodge, Montana, 18-22 October 2001; the workshop was sponsored by the Liz Claiborne-Art Ortenberg Foundation. Bill McDonald and Ron Bemis wrote a short piece that is available online: "Community Involvement and Sustainability: the Malpai Borderlands Effort" (pp. 596-603 in *Nature and Human Society: The Question for a Sustainable World*, published by the National Academy of Sciences, 1999). Kelly Cash wrote a short essay, "Malpai Borderlands: The Searchers for Common Ground," which captures the flavor of the Group well but also mythologizes it somewhat (pp. 112-121 in *Across* the Great Divide: Explorations in Collaborative Conservation and the American West, edited by Philip Brick, Donald Snow and Sarah van de Wetering, Island Press, 2001). Newspaper and magazine accounts are too numerous to list here; the major ones include the New York Times of September 24, 1996; June 14, 1998; December 26, 2000; and September 10, 2002; the Washington Post of November 13, 2004; and the June 1997 issue of Smithsonian magazine.

INTRODUCTION: THE WESTERN RANGE AND THE NEW WEST

The best recent source on the effects of population growth on ranching and rangelands in the West is Ranching West of the 100th Meridian: Culture, Ecology, and Economics, edited by Richard L. Knight, Wendell C. Gilgert, and Ed Marston (Island Press, 2003); many of the statistics I cite are from Chapter 2, "Lay of the Land: Ranch Land and Ranching," by Martha J. Sullins and three collaborators. Another general overview is William E. Reibsame's "Geographies of the New West" (pp. 45-51 in Across the Great Divide, cited above). The fact that rural residential development now occupies nearly one-quarter of the lower forty-eight states is from an article currently in press: D. G. Brown, K. M. Johnson, T. R. Loveland, and D. M. Theobald, "Rural Land Use Trends in the Coterminous U.S., 1950-2000" (Ecological Applications). Federal and state land ownership figures are from the National Wilderness Institute's website (www.nwi.org/Maps/LandChart.html, accessed 7 July 2005). For a statement of the view that eliminating the Old West from public lands will be a net environmental gain even if private lands are developed into homesites, see George Wuerthner, "Subdivisions versus Agriculture" (Conservation Biology 8(3), September 1994: 905-908). The argument that the free market will lead to environmental conservation in the New West is expressed by numerous economists and neoliberal political theorists; see especially Thomas Michael Power's Post-Cowboy Economics: Pay and Prosperity in the New American West (Island Press, 2001).

The literature on the Western Range is too large to summarize here. The name itself comes from "The Western Range: Letter from the Secretary of Agriculture in Response to Senate Resolution No. 289" (Senate Document No. 199, 74th Congress, 2nd Session, 1936). The relevant portions of the report of the Public Lands Commission can be found in "Grazing on the Public Lands" (USDA Forest Service Bulletin No. 62, 1905); the prediction-judgment that grazing would always be the highest use of the range is on the opening page. The quoted passage describing the Cattle Boom is from H.L. Bentley, "Cattle Ranges of the Southwest: A History of the Exhaustion of the Pasturage and Suggestions for Its Restoration" (USDA Farmer's Bulletin No. 72, 1898). A detailed discussion of the political maneuvering between government and the livestock industry in the first half of the twentieth century can be found in Karen R. Merrill's Public Lands and Political Meaning: Ranchers, the Government, and the Property Between Them (University of California Press, 2002).

The study of New Mexico ranch sales prices is the work of Allen Torell and various collaborators; it has not yet been published in an academic journal, but its results have been widely reported. See L. Allen Torell, Neil R. Rimbey, Octavio A. Ramirez, and Daniel W. McCollum, "New Faces and the Changing Value of Rangeland" (pp. 57-89 in Current Issues in Rangeland Resource Economics, edited by L. Allen Torell, Neil R. Rimbey, and Lynnette Harris, Utah Agricultural Experiment Station Research Report 190; accessible by link from http://ranval.nmsu.edu/).

Bernard DeVoto's column for Harper's, "The Easy Chair," took up Western land issues in January and June of 1947 and again in March 1951. He also wrote two articles on the livestock industry's post-war proposals: "The Anxious West" (December 1946, pp. 481-491) and "The West Against Itself" (January 1947, pp. 1-13; the quoted passage is on p. 12). Earlier, he had joined the debate surrounding the Taylor Grazing Act in "The West: A Plundered Province" (August 1934, pp. 355-364). DeVoto's arguments were scathing, but they were nothing compared to more recent attacks on public-lands ranching. At the informed but one-sided end of the spectrum, see Debra L. Donahue's The Western Range Revisited: Removing Livestock from Public Lands to Conserve Native Biodiversity

(University of Oklahoma Press, 1999). Donahue discusses the new, post-Clementsian findings of rangeland ecology, but her proposal to remove livestock from areas that average twelve inches or less of annual precipitation seems not to recognize that these are the lands least likely to respond to rest. She also makes erroneous claims about Southwestern rangelands: that ranchers exterminated beaver and that mesquites are non-native invaders from Mexico, for example. At the rabidly misleading end of the spectrum, see George Wuerthner and Mollie Matteson, editors, *Welfare Ranching: The Subsidized Destruction of the American West* (Island Press, 2002); for a critique of same, see my review (*Conservation Biology* 17(4), August 2003: 1186-1188).

The finding that 50 percent of ranches with federal permits are "hobby ranches" comes from Bradley J. Gentner and John A. Tanaka, "Classifying Federal Public Land Grazing Permittees" (*Journal of Range Management* 55(1), January 2002: 2-11). Grassroots efforts by ranchers and environmentalists to overcome their entrenched animosity can be found in almost every watershed in the West these days, but it was not always so. The best early account is Dan Dagget's *Beyond the Rangeland Conflict: Toward a West that Works* (Grand Canyon Trust, 1995).

CHAPTER 1: CRISIS, CONSENSUS, AND CONSERVATION

Chapters 1 and 2 are based largely on the recollections of the people involved, supplemented by archival documents. It was surprisingly difficult to pin down the chronology of events, and a number of minor details turned out to differ from what had been reported elsewhere. Whereas even Bill McDonald had written that the discussion group met for about two years, for example, the journals and datebooks of participants showed it had only lasted about nine months.

On the legal history of the San Bernardino land grant, see Ray H. Mattison, "Early Spanish and Mexican Settlements in Arizona" (*New Mexico Historical Review* 21(4), October 1946: 273-327). The selection and allocation of Arizona state trust lands is described in my *Ranching, Endangered Species, and*

Urbanization in the Southwest: Species of Capital (University of Arizona Press, 2002).

Jim Corbett's role in the Sanctuary Movement has been described in detail elsewhere; see, among other sources, Miriam Davidson's *Convictions of the Heart: Jim Corbett and the Sanctuary Movement* (University of Arizona Press, 1988). His formative influence on several other innovative social organizations is less well known. For more information, a good place to start is the Saguaro-Juniper website (www.saguaro-juniper.com). In the last years of his life, Corbett wrote a manuscript that expands and modifies the arguments contained in *Goatwalking* (Viking, 1991); that manuscript is now being published, posthumously, as *Sanctuary for All Life: the Cowbalah of Jim Corbett* (Howling Dog Press, 2005). A brief description of the Malpai discussion group meetings can be found in Sharman Apt Russell's *Kill the Cowboy: A Battle of Mythology in the New West* (Addison-Wesley, 1993).

CHAPTER 2: GRAY RANCH

The best single treatment of the Gray Ranch is George Hilliard's *A Hundred Years of Horse Tracks: The Story of the Gray Ranch* (High-Lonesome Books, 1996); most of the historical information in this chapter comes from this source. I also drew on archival materials provided to me by Wayne Pruett when I was researching the Buenos Aires Ranch; the history of that ranch and the masked bobwhite are in my *Ranching, Endangered Species, and Urbanization in the Southwest*. For the events surrounding the Gray Ranch from 1989 to 1994, see the *New York Times Sunday Magazine* of June 3, 1990; and the *Los Angeles Times* (July 21, 1991; March 21, 1993; May 19, 1996). The first John Sawhill quotation comes from the March 1993 article; the second, about "the 'museum' model of conservation," comes from Sawhill's foreword to *Two Eagles/Dos Aguilas: the Natural World of the United States-Mexico Borderlands* (photographs by Tupper Ansel Blake, text by Peter Steinhart, University of California Press, 1994). Bill McDonald's remark about Martians is from Kelly Cash's article, cited above. The Draft Environmental Assessment for the proposed Animas National Wildlife Refuge may be difficult to locate, as it was never approved and did not circulate widely; I obtained a copy courtesy of The Nature Conservancy.

CHAPTER 3: GRAZING, FIRE, AND DROUGHT IN THE BORDERLANDS

The scientific literature on these topics is vast, and there are still significant differences of opinion about many issues. I have addressed the history of Southwestern range science in greater detail elsewhere: in *Ranching, Endangered Species, and Urbanization in the Southwest* and in "The Genesis of Range Science, with Implications for Pastoral Development Policy" (with Maria Fernandez-Gimenez; pp. 1976-1985 in *Proceedings of the VIIth International Rangeland Congress*, 26 July-1 August 2003, Durban, South Africa, edited by N. Allsopp and six others). On the relationship of this history to today's landscapes and trends, see Charles G. Curtin, Nathan F. Sayre, and Benjamin D. Lane, "Transformations of the Chihuahuan Borderlands: Grazing, Fragmentation, and Biodiversity Conservation in Desert Grasslands" (*Environmental Science and Policy* 5, 2002: 55-68).

The Aldo Leopold article is in the *Journal of Forestry* 22(6), October 1924, pp. 1-10; the quoted passage occurs on page 6. The Stephen Pyne quotation is from his *World Fire: The Culture of Fire on Earth* (University of Washington Press, 1997, p. 16). For a very detailed and accessible account of the Apache period in the Borderlands, see Alden C. Hayes, *A Portal to Paradise* (University of Arizona Press, 1999). Early Anglo ranching in the area is the subject of Lynn Robison Bailey's *We'll All Wear Silk Hats: The Erie and Chiricahua Cattle Companies and the Rise of Corporate Ranching in the Sulphur Spring Valley of Arizona, 1883-1909* (Westernlore Press, 1994). For the effects of the Cattle Boom in southeastern Arizona, see Conrad J. Bahre and Marlyn L. Shelton, "Rangeland Destruction: Cattle and Drought in Southeastern Arizona at the Turn of the Century" (*Journal of the Southwest* 38(1): 1-22, 1996), and my "The Cattle Boom in Southern Arizona: Towards a Critical Political Ecology" (*Journal of the Southwest* 41(2): 239-271, 1999). The quotation from the Territorial governor is from the 1885 "Report of the Governor of Arizona to the Secretary of Interior" (Government Printing Office, 1886, pp. 6-7). Henry F. Dobyns's *From Fire to Flood: Historic Human Destruction of Sonoran Desert Riverine Oases* (Ballena Press, 1981) is somewhat dated, but it remains a good source of primary historical materials regarding arroyo formation and the question of fire. It is also one of the few attempts to deal simultaneously with fire, drought, and grazing in their historical and ecological interactions.

Key texts in early Southwestern range science include H. L. Bentley's article, cited above, and several by David Griffiths: "Range Improvement in Arizona" (USDA-Bureau of Plant Industry Bulletin No. 4, 1901); "Range Investigations in Arizona" (USDA-Bureau of Plant Industry Bulletin No. 67, 1904); and "A Protected Stock Range in Arizona" (USDA-Bureau of Plant Industry Bulletin No. 177, 1910). Griffiths published the earliest carrying capacity estimates in the 1904 report; his complaint that this was "a most difficult task" occurs on p. 32. E. O. Wooton published higher capacity estimates in 1916: "Carrying Capacity of Grazing Ranges in Southern Arizona" (USDA Bulletin No. 367). For New Mexico, see Wooton's "The Range Problem in New Mexico" (New Mexico Agricultural Experiment Station Bulletin No. 66, 1908).

The concept of carrying capacity predates Clements's classic presentation of his theory in *Plant Succession: An Analysis of the Development of Vegetation* (Carnegie Institution of Washington Publication 242, 1916) and its application to management in *Plant Indicators: The Relation of Plant Communities to Process and Practice* (Carnegie Institution of Washington Publication 290, 1920). Close reading of the latter text reveals that Clements himself did *not* advocate static carrying capacities for arid and semiarid rangelands. Arthur Sampson published many influential papers in early range science; his most famous is "Plant Succession in Relation to Range Management" (USDA Bulletin No. 791, 1919).

For accessible summaries of the latest knowledge in rangeland ecology and management, see *Rangeland Health: New Methods to Classify, Inventory, and Monitor Rangelands* (National Academy Press, 1994), and my *The New Ranch Handbook: A Guide to Restoring Western Rangelands* (Quivira Coalition, 2001).

A more detailed and scholarly treatment is *Ecological Implications of Livestock Herbivory in the West*, edited by Martin Vavra, William A. Laycock and Rex D. Pieper (Society for Range Management, 1994). The long-term measurements of forage production on the Jornada Experimental Range are analyzed in C. H. Herbel and R. P. Gibbens, "Post-Drought Vegetation Dynamics on Arid Rangelands of Southern New Mexico" (New Mexico State University Agricultural Experiment Station Bulletin 776, 1996). For a discussion of shrub encroachment in the Southwest, see Steven Archer's "Woody Plant Encroachment into Southwestern Grassland and Savannas: Rates, Patterns and Proximate Causes" (pp. 13-68 in the volume edited by Vavra, Laycock and Pieper). The estimate of acreage lost to shrub encroachment is from D. F. Gori and C. A. F. Enquist, "An Assessment of the Spatial Extent and Condition of Grasslands in Central and Southern Arizona, Southwestern New Mexico, and Northern Mexico" (report prepared by The Nature Conservancy, Tucson, 2003). References for the paragraph on the Santa Rita Experimental Range can be found in my "Recognizing History in Range Ecology: 100 Years of Science and Management on the Santa Rita Experimental Range" (pp. 1-15 in Mitchel P. McClaran, Peter F. Ffolliott, and Carleton B. Edminster, tech. coords., *Santa Rita Experimental Range: 100 Years (1903-2003) of Accomplishments and Contributions*, USDA-Forest Service, Rocky Mountain Research Station Proc. RMRS-P-30, 2003).

Robert Humphrey's views on fire can be found in *The Desert Grassland: A History of Vegetational Change and an Analysis of Causes* (University of Arizona Press, 1958) and *Range Ecology* (Ronald Press Company, 1962). The classic paper on the weaknesses of the Clementsian model and the advantages of state-and-transition models is Mark Westoby, Brian Walker, and Imanuel Noy-Meir, "Opportunistic Management for Rangelands Not at Equilibrium" (*Journal of Range Management* 42(4), July 1989: 266-274); the quotation on "vegetation changes in response to grazing" is from p. 268. An earlier paper by Westoby provides important underlying ideas: "Elements of a Theory of Vegetation Dynamics in Arid Rangelands" (*Israel Journal of Botany* 28, 1979/80: 169-194). For an excellent sum-

mary of the limits of both Clementsian and state-and-transition models, see M. Stafford Smith, "Management of Rangelands: Paradigms at Their Limits" (pp. 325-357 in *The Ecology and Management of Grazing Systems*, edited by J. Hodgson and A.W. Illius, CAB International, 1996).

CHAPTER 4: THE RADICAL CENTER: SCIENCE, POLITICS, AND PARTNERSHIPS

The best single source of information on the Malpai Group's science program is another conference proceedings volume: *Toward Integrated Research, Land Management, and Ecosystem Protection in the Malpai Borderlands: Conference Summary, January 6-8, 1999, Douglas, Arizona* (compiled by Gerald J. Gottfried, Lane G. Eskew, Charles G. Curtin, and Carleton B. Edminster, USDA-Forest Service-Rocky Mountain Research Station, Proceedings RMRS-P-10). It contains reports and research findings on all of the topics I discuss in Chapters 4-6, plus references to further sources. Here, I limit myself to references outside of this volume.

The quotation about regulations versus ranchettes is from Bill McDonald's "The Formation and History of The Malpai Borderlands Group" (pp. 483-486 in the 1994 Madrean Archipelago conference proceedings, referenced above); the passage that closes this chapter is the final paragraph of the same article. That critics of grazing considered the scientific debate to be decided is evident in a paper published the same month as the conference: Thomas L. Fleischner, "Ecological Costs of Livestock Grazing in Western North America" (*Conservation Biology* 8(3), September 1994: 629-644). Jim Brown and Bill McDonald responded the following year: "Livestock Grazing and Conservation on Southwestern Rangelands" (*Conservation Biology* 9(6), December 1995: 1644-1647).

The quotation from the 1965 edition of *The Changing Mile* (University of Arizona Press) is from p. 288. The summary statement from *The Changing Mile Revisited* (University of Arizona Press, 2003) is from p. 261; the three quotations in the subsequent paragraphs are from pp. 276-277. "Letting the chips fall where they may" is from Tom Wolf's Red Lodge case study, referenced above, where he is quoting John Cook's recollection of the words of Bill McDonald.

The Report of the Interagency Ecosystem Management Task Force is entitled "The Ecosystem Approach: Healthy Ecosystems *and* Sustainable Economies, Volume 1—Overview." It is dated June 1995 but has no publication information. Key scholarly works on adaptive management include: C. S. Holling, editor, *Adaptive Environmental Assessment and Management* (John Wiley and Sons, 1978); Carl J. Walters and Ray Hilborn, "Ecological Optimization and Adaptive Management" (*Annual Review of Ecological Systematics* 9, 1978: 157-188); and Carl J. Walters and C. S. Holling, "Large-scale Management Experiments and Learning by Doing" (*Ecology* 71(6), 1990: 2060-2068).

The Borderlands bibliography was compiled by Peter F. Ffolliott and Leonard F. DeBano: "Information on Borderlands Resources: A Bibliography for Planners, Managers, and Research Workers" (1999, accessible online at: www.rms.nau.edu/-publications/madrean/, accessed 12 July 2005). For the study on historical vegetation patterns and change, see Kevin M. Rich, Esteban Muldavin, and Thomas J. Valone, "Historical Vegetation of the Borderlands Ecosystem Management Area" (New Mexico Natural Heritage Program report, 1999); Esteban Muldavin, Teri Neville, Cathy McGuire, Philip Pearthree, and Thomas Biggs, "Soils, Geology and Vegetation Change in the Malpais [sic] Borderlands (New Mexico Natural Heritage Program report, 2002); and Esteban Muldavin, Vince Archer, and Paul Neville, "A Vegetation Map of the Borderlands Ecosystem Management Area" (New Mexico Natural Heritage Program report, 1998). Important findings of tree-ring studies can be found in: J. M. Kaib, "Fire history in riparian canyon pine-oak forests and the intervening desert grasslands of the Southwest Borderlands: A Dendroecological, Historical, and Cultural Inquiry" (masters thesis, School of Renewable Natural Resources, University of Arizona, 1998); and T. W. Swetnam and J. L. Betancourt, "Mesoscale Disturbance and Ecological Response to Decadal Climatic Variability in the American Southwest" (*Journal of Climate* 11, 1998: 3128-3147). Corrobo-

rative research based on archival sources is Conrad J. Bahre, "Wildfire in Southeastern Arizona Between 1859 and 1890" (*Desert Plants* 7(4), 1985: 190-194). For details of the wetland sediment core research, see O. K. Davis, T. Minckley, T. Moutoux, T. Jull, and B. Kalin, "The Transformation of Sonoran Desert Wetlands Following the Historic Decrease of Burning" (*Journal of Arid Environments* 50, 2002: 393-412).

Jim Brown's publications from the Portal study site are too numerous to recite here. The findings are summarized in the Curtin and Brown article referenced for the Preface; further citations are contained therein. For a discussion of fire planning on the Gray Ranch and in the Peloncillos, see my "Interacting Effects of Landownership, Land Use, and Endangered Species on Conservation of Southwestern U.S. Rangelands" (*Conservation Biology* 19(3), June 2005: 783-792). The McKinney Flats research is summarized in Charles G. Curtin, "Landscape-level Effects of Livestock on the Biodiversity of a Desert Grassland" (in the forthcoming proceedings volume from the 2004 Madrean Archipelago Conference).

CHAPTER 5: BIODIVERSITY AND ENDANGERED SPECIES

The epigraph is from the Curtin and Brown chapter in *Changing Plant Life of La Frontera*, cited above. Diana Hadley (e-mail communication) provided information on historical human settlement in the Malpai area; see also her "Grazing the Southwest Borderlands: The Peloncillo-Animas District of the Coronado National Forest in Arizona and New Mexico, 1906-1996" (pp. 93-131 in *Forests Under Fire: A Century of Ecosystem Mismanagement in the Southwest*, edited by Christopher J. Huggard and Arthur R. Gomez, University of Arizona Press, 2001). The figures on overall species richness in the region are from Richard S. Felger and Matthew B. Johnson, "Northern Sierra Madre Occidental and Its Apachian Outliers: A Neglected Center of Biodiversity" (pp. 36-59 in the proceedings volume from the 1994 conference, cited above).

The story of the Magoffins and the leopard frog is told in abbreviated fashion in Michael L. Rosenzweig's *Win-Win*

Ecology: How the Earth's Species Can Survive in the Midst of Human Enterprise (Oxford University Press, 2003). More information on the ecology and status of the leopard frog can be found in two chapters of the 1994 Madrean Archipelago conference proceedings volume: Michael J. Sredl and Jeffrey M. Howland, "Conservation and Management of Madrean Populations of the Chiricahua Leopard Frog" (pp. 379-385) and Philip C. Rosen and four others, "Introduced Aquatic Vertebrates in the Chiricahua Region: Effects on Declining Native Ranid Frogs" (pp. 251-261). For more recent information, see Philip C. Rosen and Cecil Schwalbe, "Widespread Effects of Introduced Species on Reptiles and Amphibians in the Sonoran Desert Region" (pp. 220-240 in *Invasive Exotic Species in the Sonoran Region,* edited by Barbara Tellman, University of Arizona Press and the Arizona-Sonora Desert Museum, 2002).

Further information on the ecology and management of the jaguar in the Southwest can be found in two government documents: "Conservation Assessment and Strategy for the Jaguar in Arizona and New Mexico," prepared by Terry B. Johnson and William E. Van Pelt (Technical Report 105, Nongame and Endangered Wildlife Program, Arizona Game and Fish Department, March 24, 1997); and the proposal to list the jaguar as endangered in the United States (*Federal Register* 59, 1994: 35674-35679).

The official listing of the lesser long-nosed bat can be found in the *Federal Register* of 1988 (volume 53, pp. 38456-38460). A critical analysis of the listing is E. L. Cockrum and Y. Petryszyn, "The Long-nosed Bat, Leptonycteris: An Endangered Species in the Southwest?" (*Occasional Papers,* the Museum, Texas Tech University 142, 1991:1-32). The agave research conducted in the Borderlands is presented in L. A. Slauson, "Effects of Fire on the Reproductive Biology of Agave palmeri (agavaceae)" (*Madroño* 49, 2002:1-11). On whether the bat is food-limited, see H. K. Ober, "Foraging Ecology of Lesser Long-nosed Bats" (masters thesis, School of Renewable Natural Resources. University of Arizona, 2000).

The ecology of the ridgenose rattlesnake is summarized in "Biological Opinion for the Proposed Maverick Prescribed Fire, Peloncillo Mountains, Cochise County, Arizona, and Hidalgo County, New Mexico" (U.S. Fish and Wildlife Service, Arizona Ecological Services Field Office, Phoenix, 1997). The monitoring of rattlesnakes during the Maverick burn is described in L. J. Smith, A. T. Holycross, C. W. Painter, and M. E. Douglas, "Montane rattlesnakes and prescribed fire" (*Southwestern Naturalist* 46, 2001: 54-61). For a summary and evaluation of the biologists' concerns, see H. R. Mushinsky and E. D. McCoy, "Fire, Ranching, and Endangered Species: Conflict Resolution in the Malpai Borderlands" (report to the Malpai Borderlands Group, 2003). My analysis of the breakdown in ecosystem management regarding the rattlesnake is informed by interviews with Andrew Holycross, Peter Warren, and Harry Greene.

Jim Rorabaugh's memo to his supervisors was obtained by Andrew Holycross under the Freedom of Information Act; Holycross shared it with the Malpai Group, who shared it with me. The language that effectively prohibited prescribed fires in the Peloncillo Mountains can be found in "Summary: Programmatic Biological Opinion for the Safford and Tucson Field Offices' Livestock Grazing Program, Southeastern Arizona" (U.S. Fish and Wildlife Service, Arizona Ecological Services Office, Phoenix, 1997). For a more recent statement of endangered species management issues in the region, see the "Final Biological Opinion and Conference Opinion: Continuation of Livestock Grazing on the Coronado National Forest" (U.S. Fish and Wildlife Service, Arizona Ecological Services Field Office, Phoenix, 2002).

CHAPTER 6: THE SPECTER OF SUBDIVISION

There is not room here to review the property rights literature in detail; see the discussion and references in Leigh Raymond, "Viewpoint: Are Grazing Rights on Public Lands a Form of Private Property?" (*Journal of Range Management* 50(4), July 1997: 431-438). For more on the Gray Ranch grassbank, see Drum Hadley's article, "The Origin and the Future of the Grassbank" (pp. 183-189 in *Writers on the Range,* edited by Karl Hess, Jr. and

John A. Baden, University Press of Colorado, 1998); an abridged version of the same article appeared in *Orion Afield* magazine (Winter 1998/99: 34-36). On grassbanks throughout the West, see Claire Harper, "The Grassbank™ Movement, 2001: The Status of Grassbank Initiatives in the West" (report prepared for the Conservation Fund, 2002); and the website of the National Grassbank Network (www.grassbank.net).

For a discussion of exurban and suburban development impacts on biodiversity, see Andrew J. Hansen and six others, "Effects of Exurban Development on Biodiversity: Patterns, Mechanisms, Research Needs" (*Ecological Applications*, in press). That rural residential development is a widespread phenomenon is demonstrated in David M. Theobald, "Land-use Dynamics Beyond the American Urban Fringe" (*Geographical Review* 91(3), July 2001: 544-564); for its effects on wildlife habitat, see David M. Theobald, James R. Miller, and N. Thompson Hobbs, "Estimating the Cumulative Effects of Development on Wildlife Habitat" (*Landscape and Urban Planning* 39, 1997: 25-36). The study of protected areas, ranches, and ranchettes is by Jeremy D. Maestas, Richard L. Knight, and Wendell C. Gilgert, "Biodiversity and Land-use Change in the American Mountain West" (*Geographical Review* 91(3), July 2001: 509-524). The Greater Yellowstone research can be found in: Andrew J. Hansen and nine others, "Ecological Causes and Consequences of Demographic Change in the New West" (*BioScience* 52(2), February 2002: 151-162); and Andrew J. Hansen and Jay J. Rotella, "Biophysical Factors, Land Use, and Species Viability in and around Nature Reserves" (*Conservation Biology* 16(4), August 2002: 1112-1122). On the inadequacy of public lands for biodiversity conservation in the U.S., see J. Michael Scott and five others, "Nature Reserves: Do They Capture the Full Range of America's Biological Diversity?" (*Ecological Applications* 11(4), 2001: 999-1007).

CHAPTER 7: AGAINST LONG ODDS

The quoted passage is from "Opportunistic Management for Rangelands Not at Equilibrium," p. 273 (see full citation above). For a comprehensive review of the predicament of ranching in the southwestern U.S., see *Livestock Management in the American*

Southwest: Ecology, Society, and Economics (edited by R. Jemison and C. Raish, Elsevier, 2000).

CONCLUSION: WORKING WILDERNESS

Cronon's essay is from *Uncommon Ground: Rethinking the Human Place in Nature* (Norton, 1995, pp. 69-90); the quoted passage occurs on pp. 80-81. The passage from Jim Corbett's posthumous book (cited above) is on p. 252 of the galley proofs. Holling and Meffe's article is in *Conservation Biology* 10(2), April 1996: 328-337.

PHOTOGRAPHY © AS FOLLOWS:

Valer Austin: pages 88-89

Ron Bemis: pages 7 (inset), 81

Kelly Cash: page 23

Jay Dusard: back cover (left, center), pages 2-3, 9, 14 (inset), 15 (top), 18-19, 20, 21 (both), 28, 30-31, 32, 38, 48-49, 50, 51 (both), 55, 56, 59, 60, 67, 70, 71 (all), 75, 83, 90, 91 (top), 94, 102, 110, 130, 136, 141, 145 (both), 153, 154, 160, 161 (both)

Jack Dykinga: pages 12-13, 14 (top), 62, 65, 104-105, 106-107 (top), 122

Warner Glenn: 107 (top inset), 112, 127, 135

W. Ross Humphreys: pages 1, 4-5, 11, 15 (inset), 17, 27, 33 (inset), 43, 46, 68-69, 73, 76, 79, 85, 86, 87, 91 (inset), 98, 107 (lower inset), 115, 121, 124-125, 126-127 (top), 131, 133, 134, 138, 140, 142-143, 144, 146, 149, 150, 157, 158-159, 164

Malpai Borderlands Group: 109

Will van Overbeek: back cover (right), pages 24, 33 (top), 97

William R. Radke: front cover, pages 6-7, 45, 116

Ray Turner: page 53

Sterling Vinson: page 40

Bob Webb: page 93

All maps (pages 35, 36, 119, and 129) created by Darin Jensen, with help from Don Bain. Historical photo on page 10 courtesy of Southwest Studies, Maricopa Community College; historical photo on page 52 courtesy of U.S. Geological Survey Photographic Library (photo by A. T. Schwennesen, #23).

INDEX

Page numbers in *italic* type indicate illustrations.

Abbott, Jim, 97, 101, 103

Agave palmeri, 114, 123

Allen, Larry, *9, 97*, 103

Animas Foundation, 52, 63-64, 103, 130-131, 145-146

Animas National Wildlife Refuge. *See* Gray Ranch

Arizona Game and Fish Department, 113

Austin, Josiah and Valer, *9, 98*-99

Babbitt, Bruce, 90

bat, lesser long-nosed, 114-116, 123

Bell, Gary, 58

Bemis, Ron, *9, 46, 97*, 103, 126

Bentley, H. L., 22

biodiversity. *See under* Borderlands

Bonniver, Guy, 58

Borderlands

    biodiversity and ecology, 7-8, 33-34, 37, 46, 72-74, 106-117, 120-121, 123, 139-141, 156, 163

    description, 162-163

    economy, 20-22, 24-25

    history, 72-75

    population growth, 20-21

Brenner, Pablo, 56-57

Brown, Ben, *9*, 59, 146

Brown, Jim, 99-101, 145

Buenos Aires National Wildlife Refuge, 57

Buenos Aires Ranch, 56-57

Bureau of Land Management, 23, 41

carrying capacities. *See* stocking rates

Cash, Kelly, 146

Center for Biological Diversity, 152, 154

Clark, Jamie, 114

Clements, Frederic, 78

climax communities, 78

conservation, community-based, 151

conservation easements, 8, 128-132, 134-135, 137, 155-156

conservation ranching, 63-64

Cook, John, *9, 59*-61, 63, 65-66, 84, 113, 137, 151

Corbett, Jim, *40*-42, 44, 65, 151, 163-164

Cottonwood Allotment, 84-86

Curetin, Dale, 160-162

Curtin, Charles, 100-101

Darnell, Billy, *9, 131*

Day, Tom, *56*

Dennis, Mike, *9*, 59, 66, 132, 137

development. *See* subdivision and development

DeVoto, Bernard, 25-26

Diamond A Ranch. *See* Gray Ranch

drought, 74-75, 80, 83, 131-132, 134, 163

Dunagan, David, *87*

Dwyer, Don, *9*

easements, conservation. *See* conservation easements

economics. *See under* Borderlands; ranching

ecosystem management, 95-97, 99-103

Edminster, Carl, 97

Elbrock, Edward, 132-*133*, 134

endangered species, 103, 106-117, 120-121, 123

    See also bat, lesser long-nosed; frog, Chiricahua leopard; jaguar; rattlesnake, New Mexico ridgenose

Endangered Species Act, 118, 120, 149

fire

    benefits of, 39-40, 46, 71, 73-74, 81, 115-116

    and endangered species, 109, 116-117

    management, 45-47, 70-72, 101, 118, 120

    restoration, 8, 127, 155, 162

    suppression, 6-7, 44-45, 47, 54, 78-80, 94-95, 118, 162-163

fires
    Baker I, 101-103, 114, 118-120
    Baker II, 117-120
    Geronimo Trail Road, 6, 39-40, 44, 119, 160-162
    Maverick, 114-120, 123
frog, Chiricahua leopard, 110-111, 120-121, 123, 145

Glenn, Kelly, 161
Glenn, Warner and Wendy, *9*, 10, *24*, 32, 40, 44, 46-47, 66,
    95, 112-113, *136-137*, 145, 148, 161
grassbanking, 130-135, 145
Gray Ranch, 7-8, 34, 37, 47, 50-66, 115-116, 118, 130-131,
    145
    description, 50, 53, 63
    ecology and history, 53-55, 58
    management areas, 60-61
    management by and sale to Animus Foundation, 52, 63-64
    McKinley Flats study, 100-101
    proposed as Animus National Wildlife Refuge, 57
    sale to corporations, 54
    sale to Nature Conservancy, 51, 57-58
grazing. *See also* overgrazing
    leases, 128, 132, 152, 155-156
    limitations on federal lands, 25-26
    seasonal, 86-87
Guadalupe Canyon Ranch, 38-39

Habitat Conservation Plan, 149-150
Hadley, Drummond "Drum," *9*, *38*-42, 45-47, 52, 61, 63, 65-
    66, 84, 101, *130*, 138, 145
Hadley, Seth, *9*, 63
Hasting, Rodney, 94-95
Hearst, George, 37
Holling, C. S., 162
Holycross, Andrew, 120
Homestead Act, 37
homesteading, 22-23

Humphrey, Robert, 81
Humphreys, Ross, *9*

Interagency Ecosystem Management Task Force, 95

jaguar, 111-114, 121, 145
Jornada Experimental Range, 75-76, 78, 80

Kern County Land Company, 54
Kimble, Donnie, 17, *18-19*
Krentz, Carrie, 148
Kreutz, Phil, Ben, and Rob, *150*

land ownership, 22-23, 34, 36-37, 65-66, 128
land use, 22-26
Lasher, Danielle, *131*

Magoffin, Matt and Anna, *75*, 84, 111, *121*, 145
Malpai Borderlands Group
    Agenda for Grazing in the Sonoran and Chihuahuan
    Bioregions, 42-44, 66, 87, 145, 164
    incorporation, 66
    mission statement, 8, 108, 151
    organizational meetings, 40-42, 44-47, 149
    planning area, 34
Marks, D. S., 70
McDonald, Bill, 8, *9*, 46-47, 57-58, 64-66, 84-*85*, 86-87, 95,
    103, 113, 135, 137, 146, 150-151
McDonald, Mary, *9*, 47, 66, 148
McDonald, Sarah, *79*
McKinney Flats study, 100-101
McPherson, Guy, 46
Meffe, Gary, 162
mesquite. *See* shrub encroachment
Miller, Bill, *9*, *146*
monitoring ecological change, 147-148
Moore, Lonnie, 57-58

Nature Conservancy, 41, 47, 51-52, 57-61, 63-66, 103, 145
Newlands Act, 22
New Mexico Game and Fish Department, 114
Noy-Meir, Imanuel, 156

overgrazing, 22, 25-26, 29, 42, 54, 77-80, 163

Pacific Western Land Company, 54
Palmer's agave. *See Agave palmeri*
Parker, Kenneth, 80-81
Pérez, Ignacio, 34
Peterson, Tom, *9*
photography, repeat, *52-53*, 92-93
public lands. *See* land ownership
Public Lands Commission, 22-25

Rabinowitz, Alan, 113
rainfall, 22, 82-84, 101
Ramsey, Walter, 39
ranching
    criticism of, 25-26, 39, 90-91, 144
    economics, 24, 26, 152
    subsidies, 26
    tax shelter, 54-55
rangeland
    conditions, 22, 25, 33, 46
    development. *See* subdivision and development
    management, 75-78, 86
    reform, 90-91, 95
    remediation, 29, 155
range science, 82, 87
rattlesnake, New Mexico ridgenose, 114, 116-117, 123
regulation, federal, 22-23, 25
Roos, Ed, *9, 86*
Rorabaugh, Jim, 117, 120
Rosen, Phil, *75*

Sagebrush Rebellion, 25
Saguaro-Juniper Association, 41
Sampson, Arthur, 78
San Bernardino National Wildlife Refuge, 34, 111
San Bernardino Ranch, 34, 51, 136
Santa Rita Experimental Range, 75-76, 80-81
Sawhill, John, 51, 59, 64, 145
Schwalbe, Cecil, *75*
Selcraig, Bruce, 57
shrub encroachment, 39, 46, *52-53*, 54, 74, 77, 80-82, 95,
    100-101, 108, 134, 154-155, 160-163
Slaughter, John, 34, 37, 84
Southwestern Borderlands Ecosystem Management Project,
    97, 99-103
stocking rates, 23-24, 26, 29, 75-80, 82, 156, 162
subdivision and development, 22, 126-130, 132, 134, 136,
    138-141
Sundt, Pete, 148
Sycamore Ranch, 84

Taylor Grazing Act, 23, 37
Tenneco West, 54
Turner, Ted, 61
Turner, Ray, *9*, 42, 46-47, 52, *92-93*, 94-95, 145

Unger, David, 103
U.S. Fish and Wildlife Service, 112-115, 117, 120, 123, 150
U.S. Forest Service, 114

Victorio Land and Cattle Company, 54-56

Warren, Peter, *115*
Walker, Brian, 156
Walter, Wart, *134*
Warren, Peter, 148
water resources, 34, 37
Westerm Range, 22-26, 28-29, 77, 82, 92, 96, 128, 139, 149,
    154, 156-157

Western Range, New, 145, 155-157
Westoby, Mark, 156
Winkler, Mary, 133-*134*
Woodling, Reese, 146, 148-*149*
working wilderness, 160-164